HIGHWAYS AND HEDGES

New Life Lessons from a Trail Chaplain

BRAD "SHEP" SASSER

CONTENTS

To everyone who saved their lunch money for the book fair.

To anyone who reads on lunch break.

To everyone who hopes to make a difference in this life.

INTRODUCTION

"Then the Master said to the servant, Go out into the highways and hedges, and compel them to come in, that my house may be filled."

— LUKE 14:23 NKJV

It's been nearly one year since I sat down to write *The Road Less Traveled: 23 Life Lessons From the Trail.* Due to the overwhelming positive response, and taking your feedback into account, I'm extremely happy to bring you another volume. Some have wondered how I come up with material, and what the process looks like. Truthfully, I never go out looking for ideas. I never start my day wondering what will turn out to make a good story, or what the spiritual connection is. We just live life and before long things are jumping out at me.

One thing that jumps out is, I believe we misinterpret large portions of our life. We fail to see the miraculous happening all around us, and perhaps miss the lessons God is trying to teach. That doesn't make us bad; it makes us human. The disciples constantly misinterpreted what Jesus was trying to teach them. They looked at life lessons through the lens of everyday Jewish culture of the time. Christ was trying to get them to step into a different place, and see with open eyes the lessons he was teaching so they could see the deeper meaning He was attempting to convey. I believe He is still trying to bring us to this place today. So come along with me on another journey, as I attempt to share new lessons I've learned from the trail.

I'm one sent to the highways and hedges to compel others to come. My stories are born out of this desire to share what I've been given. I'm not special, there are others like me, better than me, all over the world. However, in an attempt to understand my calling and motivation we will start from the beginning.

"I freely admit that I am a bit of a misfit."

— RHYS IFANS

It was a hot summer night in mid-July; the kind of night that sweat makes your shirt stick to you uncomfortably. My nervous excitement made my palms even more sweaty. We were laying in the grass alongside Hwy 51, the main thoroughfare that runs through Barbour County, Alabama. This night we were waiting to see how many cars would stop at our makeshift roadblock. Yep, a few teenage boys, and a couple "borrowed" road cones equals shutting down the highway this July night. We trembled with a mix of fear and youthful exuberance. Cars began to stop, lines formed, people got out to look around, and finally the town cop came to throw the cones out of the road. We ducked our heads low as he shined his spotlight around the grassy field, and then he drove away. We had done it. Another successful night in southeast

Alabama; not the first time we had pulled a stunt like this, nor the last.

I could tell at least fifty stories of similar exploits, the kind of stories that make you smile twenty years later, and the ones that still make your momma gasp. I looked up the statute of limitations before deciding that I could publish any of this, so I promise to only incriminate myself. I won't tell the one about the golf cart, the first time we ever laid eyes on a zero turn lawn mower, the old Dixie Academy school bus, or our love for campaign signs. However, I will say that campaign signs, when collected and placed by the dozens in selected yards, can make a great Saturday morning surprise.

If you haven't figured it out yet, I grew up in small town U.S.A. For the most part we had a lot of good natured fun. Thankfully, we lived through it. I was a church going kid, as were most of my friends. We might burn it down on Saturday, but our parents made sure we were in church on Sunday. I was just good enough to get by, until getting by wasn't good enough.

In college I excelled in academics. This was an amazing accomplishment given the track record of my early high school years. However in my latter collegiate career, I was failing fast at life. I was one of those kids who was fairly good, because I'd never had the opportunity to be bad. **When moments of opportunity cross paths with spiritual weakness there is always chaos**. The good natured fun turned dark; day drinking on a Tuesday, and riding electric bulls in honky tonks. Even my friends in low places started to look down on me. Good folks told their daughters to watch out for me, and people refused to let me drive anywhere. After college graduation, I was satisfied working my part time job at the local grocery store, where I was affectionately known as "Flunky."

I was not at the front of the line to live a life of service to Christ and others. I was much closer to the back than anyone now seems to remember. There is a simple term to describe that version of me; I was a MISFIT.

I am glad that Christ seems to have an inclination for misfits. As a matter of fact, when reading scripture, you see the who's who of the Bible is a who's who of misfits. Those used in the Bible are literally citizens of the Island of Misfit Toys. God uses misfits to change the world. You know the stories, but I'll give you a rundown. Moses was a murderer hiding on the backside of the desert. Jonah ran from the call and ended up being consumed by a great fish. Matthew was a hated member of the establishment; a tax collector. Peter was temperamental. There's Paul, known as Saul, who sent Christians to prison and death, and then centuries later, way down the list, there's me.

I remember when God began to drop subtle hints of the call on my life. The first one came in college. I was in a leadership class my sophomore year at Troy University. We had a guest come in, who was tasked with administering the Myers Briggs Personality Test to the class of around fifty students. I did my best to answer each question honestly and accurately. I had no clue what this test would say with no preconceived notions, but I did know I wanted to be a lawyer, or a military officer. I hoped at the end, my results would confirm all my suspicions, that I would become the next great southern trial lawyer. I already envisioned myself drinking sweet tea on the back patio of my antebellum home under the oaks weighed low with Spanish moss. I wanted to be that backwoods southern lawyer you could trust.

Worst case scenario I was sure it would tell me that I was bound for a military career. Yes, I'd have a couple stars on my shoulder, and have lots of adventures. This was pre 9/11 and military life was still a romantic notion. This was kind of the family business on my dad's side of the family. For sure, in the worst case, I'd be heading to the United States Army OCS (Officer Candidate School) directly after graduation. There you have it, my plans, but sometimes God has other plans.

They took our scantrons and ran them through the machine giving us scores that corresponded to one of sixteen different personality types. I should have known something was up when the proctor asked us who fell into the INFJ box; I was so preoccupied with my sweet tea, spanish moss daydreams, I almost missed the question. Exactly two of us in the fifty person classroom raised our hands. The instructor smiled and said congrats. You two have the rarest of all personality types and began passing out papers which listed the job types people with our personalities usually gravitate towards. I remember thinking I must be right, after all, everyone can't be uber successful backwoods southern lawyers. He said my type was rare. I got this in the bag.

I sat looking at my paper in stunned silence. I remember some of the job titles: Social Worker, Librarian, Writer, School Counselor, Social Scientist, Pastor, Missionary, Humanitarian Aid Worker. What?? On average INFJ's have the lowest annual salary of all sixteen personality types. Do Humanitarian Aid Workers even get paid? While others shared freely with excitement the results of their test, I sank into my seat. I was so selfish in this time period that all I could think about was how much I disliked my results. It was as if a pin had burst the little daydream bubble over my head. Pastor, missionary; they have got to be kidding. Obviously my results got mixed up.

I had a friend from high school who took this test. He was absolutely the best Christian guy I knew growing up. He mentioned his results and told me some of the possible jobs that his paper listed: Engineer, Architecture, Computer Science, Military Officer, Business Administration, basically all the stuff I wanted. I remember telling him that we must have gotten mixed up because I had his paper and he had mine.

The second time God revealed his plans was more apparent. There was a group of us standing outside of our church one Sunday evening. Now understand, the main reasons I went to church at this point was to impress girls, see what friends would be there, and make plans with these friends to go eat after church. Having to actually attend service was something I obliged because it was bad etiquette to show up just as the church let out.

As we stood there, probably debating if we would go to Troy and eat Chinese, or Ozark and eat Mexican, my aunt came over and informed the whole group that she had a dream. She said in the dream I was speaking to an auditorium full of people, a church somewhere, and she was sure it meant I was called to preach the Gospel. I assured her that couldn't possibly be what the dream meant, and if we'd have taken a poll, I don't think anyone else thought it was possible. We were the town misfits after all.

However, like the biblical accounts, **there will come a**

time when the misfits meet the Maker. For Moses this was while he was keeping Jethro's flock and spied a burning bush. For Matthew the moment came while he was collecting taxes, and for Saul it happened on the Damascus road. For Brad Sasser that moment was a Sunday night revival in a little Assembly of God church in Blue Springs, Alabama.

I distinctly remember I was living according to standards far below the life I should have been living. I had days with thoughts similar to the prodigal son who was eating pig scraps. Most folks in this condition will not admit it, but they are miserable because they are attempting to fit into a world they aren't made for. You go to church miserable because God convicts, and you go to the party miserable because you know deep down you don't belong in that place. It was this condition of misery I found myself living. I knew something had to give; something had to change.

Michelle, my beautiful wife, was a co-worker at the time, and the pastor's daughter. She invited me to the revival at their church. I'd managed to get myself banned from ever spending time with her, but she figured the only way around that was to invite me to church. I found myself sitting on the second row of a little Pentecostal church at a revival on a Sunday night. Now, for those of you that don't know, this is a very dangerous place to be if you are struggling as I was. The back row is much safer, and it's closer to the door, in case you need to make a quick break for the parking lot. But Michelle sat with her family on the second row. She was beautiful, and had invited me. I was young and dumb.

I don't remember everything about that night, but the

Evangelist was someone I've never forgotten, Bro. David Copeland. I'd never heard anyone preach like that; I didn't know that much passion and energy could reside in a person. When the altar call was given I believe I floated to the front of that church. I remember praying for forgiveness, repenting of my crazy ways, and being slightly afraid to look up as the evangelist came by praying for people. What a night. I had clearly heard a "follow me" and I was ready to see what the future might hold.

Truth be told we all have a little "misfit" in us. Likewise, many have felt the gentle nudge of the Lord and had to make a choice. Do you settle into the pre prescribed roles like shepherd, tax collector, religious zealot, or small town misfit? Or, do you hear the call of God and venture out into the roles he has for you?

LESSON #1
FREEDOM FROM FEAR

He who is not everyday conquering some fear has not learned the secret of life.

— RALPH WALDO EMERSON

The beauty and uniqueness of Shady Valley, Tennessee has been well documented. The valley, once covered in trees - hence the name - is now an aging farming community. Some barns along the main highway date back to the era just after the Civil War. I often look at these relics of another time, and wonder what types of stories they'd tell if they could talk. No doubt one could sit for hours and listen to stories of hanging tobacco, haystacks the size of small houses, and barefoot little boys full of mischief. And while Johnson County has been immortalized for moonshine production in songs like "Copperhead Road," Shady Valley is a completely dry community to this day. Another interesting fact, the Shady Valley post office is known as the highest post office in Tennessee. The post office sits at an elevation of 2,785 feet above sea level, and that brings me to my topic.

What does a post office have to do with fear? It's a funny story. Michelle and I decided that we needed the ability to receive mail while we are in Tennessee. We were a little surprised when we realized this was a much smaller post office than we were accustomed to using. There were only 119 boxes available for rent in a community of several hundred people, which did not bode well for us. These boxes were not the type you used a key with, these were old school, gold boxes with a little tinted window and a fancy combination knob. I thought to myself, "I'll never be able to get into these type boxes if they happen to have one open for rent."

The young man behind the counter was a friendly fellow. We told him we wanted to rent a box if one was free. "Well let me see, I do have one open box" he said with a pause. "Is there any chance you'll take box 13?" Michelle and I looked at one another, no reason why we wouldn't take thirteen. "Folks around here are a little superstitious, afraid of that box" chimed our new friend. Oh well, thirteen will be just fine for us.

Superstition and fear is nothing new for me. Growing up in the deep south I was well versed in the old tales. I knew we didn't do laundry on New Year's Day, we painted porches "haint blue" to ward off evil spirits, and if you had a sudden chill someone was walking on your grave. Yep, and if you moved you had to buy a new broom, it was bad luck to go bringing in dirt from the past to a new place. Then there was the dreaded black cat. I always laughed when I got into a car and saw the fingerprint mark of an

"X" on the front windshield. You had to do that "X" if a solid black cat ran across the road in front of you, or so the superstition goes. Where does this stuff come from?

You see, that's the thing with fear, the majority of what we fear has no real basis in reality. We get worked up over things that should have no control over us. Ninety percent of the things we worry about never come to pass, and as mentioned above, some of the things we fear are just ludicrous.

There is so much information available on finding freedom from fear that some of this will be repetitive. I'm sure there are authors who have written on this subject before, but fear, anxiety, and worry seem to be pervasive in our culture, and nobody is immune. So I'd like to give you five practical steps to find freedom from fear in your life.

First, you must know who you have with you. I remember once while hiking on the Pinhoti Trail in Alabama my hiking partner and I went into a little country store. Now, when I say country please understand me, this place buys gold and silver, does taxidermy, and the fellow behind the counter had a huge six shot pistol on his side. This place was fried chicken and cornbread southern, and my hiking friend had spent a good bit of time living up north. I jokingly told him not to go into stores like that without me. "Were we in danger?" he asked "Nope," I said with a laugh, "but just for good measure." Sometimes we find ourselves in fearful situations, but we can relax when we have someone with us who understands the situation.

For me, as a Christian, I clearly hear the words of Isaiah 41:10, "Fear not, for I am with you; be not dismayed, for I am your God; I will strengthen you, I will help you, I will uphold you with my righteous right hand."[1] Fear not,

I'm going with you. What a beautiful promise from the Lord. I have someone with me who understands the situation. If it's a disease, He is my healer, if it's worry He is my peace. The important thing to remember is He is with us. When fear comes in, cling to the presence of God!

Next, understand that fear is not from God. 2 Timothy 1:7 tells us, "For God has not given us a Spirit of fear, but of power and of love and of a sound mind."[2] It is a natural human response to experience fear. Science will tell you it comes from the years man spent living in lower parts of the food chain. Most likely it has to do with the uncertain existence we live in a world marred by sin, but fear happens. When it happens we must realize it isn't from God. Fear and faith seem to work counter to one another. When fear goes up, faith seems to wane, and when faith goes up, fear begins to fall. Know that God has promised you a clear, strong mind unabated by fear and worry. Clear your mind, focus on your blessings, share love, and watch fear melt away.

Love is a key to finding freedom in fear. We all have people who love us and want the best for us. If you read this and don't feel you have these people please feel free to contact my wife and I. That's what we do, we love people. Find people who love you, and let them love you. Just knowing that there are people in your corner who care, people who are praying, people who love you, is enough to put fear to flight. When love comes, fear leaves. Remember, 1 John 4:18 says "There is no fear in love, but perfect love casts out fear."[3]

My fourth point is likely the one you were thinking about from the beginning. Matthew 6:34 says, "Do not worry about tomorrow for tomorrow will worry about itself." Simply put, don't borrow from tomorrow. If there is one point I struggle with the most, it is this. Sometimes it seems my mind doesn't turn off, I'm constantly calculating, doing the math, and preparing for tomorrow. While this can be a smart thing to do; it can lead to the propensity for worrying about tomorrow. The Bible is clear, don't worry about tomorrow.

A recent study at Penn State University uncovered only 1 in 10 things we worry about actually come to pass. They asked twenty nine people with General Anxiety Disorder to write down everything they worried about over a ten day period. Then they asked them how many of those worries came true over the course of the next thirty days. The results were interesting. 91.4% of the worries participants stated did not come to pass.[4] Don't waste your time borrowing from tomorrow.

Finally, you must cast all your anxiety on the Lord. 1 Peter 5:7 says to cast, not carry. We carry our anxiety, become beaten down from oppressive worry over our anxiety, and stay up late at night tribulating over everything. Why do we cast our cares on the Lord? It's because he cares for us. God does not slumber or sleep, give your cares to him and get some rest. I know that sounds like an oversimplification, but so many things in the kingdom are simple. We overcomplicate things when childlike faith is what is needed.

I am not perfect and can't say I live free from worry, fear, and anxiety. Honestly, I doubt anyone alive can say they go long periods of time without the worry monster raising its head, but rest assured, remembering these five pieces of advice will help us find the freedom from fear we need.

. . .

<u>Reflection</u>

1. Are you carrying any fear in your life right now?
   Not succeeding? Having no money?
   Relationship issues? If yes, specifically define
   the fear.
2. Spend time in prayer and applying the five steps
   to overcoming fear. Afterward, how do you feel?
   Do you have release from fear and anxiety?
3. "Fear not" is mentioned 365 times in the Bible,
   and fear is mentioned around 500 times. Use a
   reference Bible, concordance, or other study
   material to gain a deeper understanding of what
   scripture says about fear. Write out the verses
   that give you comfort.

LESSON #2
THE JOURNEY OR THE DESTINATION?

"The man who enjoys the walk will go further than the man who enjoys the destination."

— ANONYMOUS

I'm so very blessed to be able to do life with, and minister to, some of the most amazing individuals. They come from every walk of life, every corner of the globe, and every belief system. We have crazy trail names, sing silly songs, and sleep in the dirt. Our legs hurt, toenails fall off, and some people wonder why we do it. Yes the mountains are beautiful, nature is amazing, but I think most people will tell you they really enjoy the camaraderie, the characters, and the people they meet along the way.

Often I feel like Forrest Gump when he is giving the rundown of all the guys he's serving with in Vietnam and where they are from. There's Treefrog from Memphis, Flint from Detroit, and Tex; well I don't really know where Tex is from. I'm thankful the Lord blessed me with a good memory because of the plethora of trail names, real names, faces, and places I find myself having to keep straight.

I enjoy sharing trail stories from time to time, and I feel that sometimes people think I'm telling fish tales. I'll talk about sleeping in my car next to the same friends for several nights. I fold up the backseat of my truck and sleep behind my driver's seat. My buddy lays the front seat of his car back with a towel in the window for privacy, while someone else is sleeping on a mat underneath a Jeep with a lift kit. I'll mention the trail names, talk about cooking trout over fires, and remark that this was probably how Jesus did it at the end of John's gospel. Then I realize I'm losing my audience. This way of life is so foreign to most; this manner of living so primitive and scary.

"Brad must be making this up, this really can't all be true, surely he is embellishing some of these larger than life characters." I told my wife that when I die my funeral will look like the ending scene from the movie *Big Fish*. There will be characters showing up people never believed were real until they met them at the very end.

Every day we trust that God will place the right people in our path. Recently, Michelle and I told the kids we were going hiking to see who we'd run into. On the way up the mountain to Low Gap we met a hiker walking down the roadside towards Shady Valley. I immediately turned around, I needed to see where he was headed and if we could help. He told me he was going to take a road walk to Damascus, which was about eleven miles. I slid the kids over and we gave him a ride to Damascus instead. This was a much safer option than him walking on the side of a busy mountain road.

We learned his trail name was Sage as he described his journey, which included no hiking experience, and he told us of the loss he experienced in his life. I concluded he was a good guy that had accomplished a ton to get this far as a novice hiker with no apps or maps, and we dropped him off. I believed we would see our new friend again, and I was correct.

The next day we were in the Damascus town park. We had the team from Southeastern University (SEU) with us and we were being interviewed for a news article. I spotted Sage and asked if he wanted to eat lunch but he'd already eaten. When the Lord allows me to cross paths with the same person multiple times I always try to be sensitive to the Spirit in these interactions. What is the need in this individual's life? How can I be a blessing to them?

Later that evening we were back at the lot in Shady Valley eating dinner. I glanced up, and who did I see walking down the road past the lot? My buddy Sage. I called him over and found out he was road walking to Mountain City after getting a hitch from Damascus. This road is worse than the previous road for traffic and curves so I told him to camp with us and I'd take him to Mountain City the next day. After dinner we gathered by the campfire and reflected on the best things that had happened in our day, and we sang worship songs. The next day as we drove I shared with our new friend, and asked what he thought about our campfire session. He told me the main thing was peace; so much peace in that time by the fire. Remember, it's the people we meet and the interactions we have, that make a difference.

So there's the age old question, "Is life about the journey or the destination?" I have always enjoyed this debate, but also wonder why questions must have an "either or" answer. Is it the journey or the destination? It can't be both; it must be one or the other. It's kind of like the chicken or the egg debate. Which came first? It must be one or the other, but what if the answer is not as cut and dry as we'd like it to be?

For sure the journey is important. I lived many years not sure what my journey on this earth was supposed to look like. I don't think I was outside of God's will for my life in my previous ministry assignments, but I was miserable at times in my day to day living. It's unfortunate that many of us don't ever really enjoy this one beautiful life our Creator has granted us. I hope we all find things we enjoy doing, and do those things as much as we can as long as it doesn't conflict with Scripture. If you enjoy weeding your garden, and that brings you joy and fulfillment, then weed the garden as often as you can. I'm a huge proponent of fun. I like to think I have about as much fun as one can have and still make Heaven. Unfortunately, some Christians believe God put us on earth to tribulate as much as possible, and look like we've eaten sour grapes. God is not mad at you if you have fun! Life can be hard enough without us purposefully being mad at the world. Ride four wheelers in the mud, go fishing, climb mountains, jump off waterfalls, and let your hair down. Let your journey be filled with joy and have a little fun.

We recently had a wonderful group of students from SEU visit, and work alongside us for a week. We fed hikers, got into meaningful conversations, served food at hostels, removed over a ton of trash from our lot, and had a free day reserved for fun. We went white water rafting, and then traveled over to Gatlinburg to the candy store, because Gatlinburg and Pigeon Forge are Las Vegas for Christians. It was so much fun! You can love and serve the Lord, and have fun doing it. Enjoy your journey.

The destination. If you have a Biblical view of things then you know there is a destination at the end of this thing. I personally do not believe this life is the end of all things. Do I claim to be an expert on eschatology (big word that has to do with the study of death, judgment, and the afterlife)? Absolutely not, but I am fully convinced that 2 Corinthians is correct in saying, "To be absent from the body is to be present with the Lord." If you believe in God or not, sometime in the next one hundred years, everyone reading these words will meet Him. That's why faith and belief in Christ, and His sacrifice are important, because we have no hope in our final destination without it. Enjoy the journey, and prepare for the destination.

So, what makes the question not as cut and dry as an "either or answer?" I gave you my answer before I ever asked the question. James Norbury sums it up well in his book *Big Panda and Tiny Dragon*. The book uses illustrations to promote mindfulness and healthy thinking. One illustration shows the tiny dragon riding on the big panda's back. Big panda asks the question, "What is more important, the journey or the destination?" Dragon replies, "The company."[1] Ah, so much truth in such a simple statement.

In the middle of your personal life journey, and the destination you are heading, lie all the people we meet along the way. Many hikers are quick to tell you, it's about the people they meet. Life is so much more fun when shared with others. Sure, I could have fun floating down a river by myself, but it's so much better with six or seven friends. It is always my goal to add value to the life of every person we encounter on the trail. I want people to walk away uplifted and encouraged, every time. This was the example Jesus gave us.

Christ always took time to invest in people. Take a look at the story of Zacchaeus in Luke 19. You probably already know the story; Zacchaeus was a tax collector. This meant he cheated his neighbors, and lived a life of excess. The Bible says he was short so he climbed a Sycamore tree to see Jesus as he was passing by. As Christ came by He looked up and told Zacchaeus to come down, He was going to be a guest in His house today. A Rabbi going to be a guest in the house of a sinner? How shameful many in the crowd thought aloud, but Christ was willing to go out of His way to spend time with someone who was hated. Zaccaehus believed he was the Messiah and his life was changed that day.

The actions of Jesus go even further to illustrate His ability to defy prejudice, and show love to others. The Gospel of John (chapter 4) teaches us the story of the woman at the well. Not just any woman; a Samaritan woman. Jews looked down on Samaritans, and some refused to even step foot into the land of Samaria due to long standing prejudice. Christ deliberately walked through Samaria and came to a well around mid-day, and there he encountered a woman. She was coming to draw water, but why was she coming in the hottest part of the day? Most women got up early and came in the morning before the deep heat of mid-day, but this particular woman was ashamed of her life and was ostracized by the other women. Once again, at this time, it was shameful for a Rabbi to speak to a single woman. Just like the story of Zaccaehus, Jesus was willing to be looked down upon in order to raise another up. He offers her living water, tells her she will never thirst again, and asks her to go and get her husband. She shamefully looks at the ground and says she has no husband, to which Christ replies, "Yes, you have had five husbands, and the man you are with now is not your husband." Ultimately she believes He is the Savior they've looked for and runs to tell the village, "Come see a man who told me everything I've done."

Then, we have the disciples. These twelve men were a motley crew of fellows for sure. You had possibly six fishermen, a tax collector, and a Zealot among the group of twelve. Matthew, the tax collector, did the bidding of the Roman government, while Zealots carried daggers and swore that they would assassinate anyone who sided with Rome. I can imagine Matthew slept with one eye open many nights hoping that Simon the Zealot was really all in on loving and following the Messiah. If not, it was possible he wouldn't make morning. In the middle of this group was Jesus, living and teaching them for three years. Sowing into their lives, knowing that what they would become was so much greater than who they were in those opening years. Jesus invested in people.

Jesus invested in Judas. I don't believe Christ ever treated Judas any differently than anyone else, even though Judas would eventually betray Him. Actually, Jesus treated him better in some regards. Judas was allowed to be the keeper of the money purse. He had a little responsibility that others in the group lacked. Also, at the last supper Jesus identifies the traitor by sharing food with him. Sharing food was an indication of friendship and peace in the ancient world.

Jesus knew that one of the best parts of this journey

are the people we meet, the companions we travel with, and the ones we uplift along the way. I encourage you to never waste a moment you're given to invest into the life of another. Jesus loved the have nots and the not yets, and hopefully we do too.

<u>Reflection</u>

1. What are things you enjoy doing that bring you joy? How can you incorporate more of these activities into your journey?
2. Do you take time to invest in the lives of others? Reflect on a recent interaction that allowed you to bless another.
3. Take a few moments to reflect on individuals who invested in your life.
4. Who are a few friends you enjoy spending time with? Make sure you let them know what they mean to you.

LESSON #3
THE RIGHT PLACE, AT THE RIGHT TIME

"The meaning of life is to find your gift. The purpose of life is to give it away."

— PABLO PICASSO

As missionary Chaplains we can never do what we do for others without help. So many folks bless us with their prayers, financial giving, and occasionally with items we need. Our friends, Pastors Josh and Kayla Simms, asked us if we had any needs, anything they could help us purchase. We were in the process of gathering supplies for the 2022 thru hikers and foot care needs were a must. Our friends helped us order the Leuko tape, small triple antibiotic ointments, and bandages.

I mentioned in my previous book how important it is to take proper care of your feet. When I started my walk across Alabama I didn't have a clue and my feet suffered. This is the story with many beginning thru hikers. They have new shoes that aren't properly broken in, which cause blisters, boots that are too big or too small, which cause blisters, and the general wear and tear of tender new feet. Believe me, blisters can shut down a thru hike attempt in an instant.

I learned a few lessons this past year hiking the FLorida Trail. I'm past getting blisters in the mountains. I've got that dialed in. However, a new environment like Florida trashed my feet. Walking in water, on sand, back to water, then on the road was a grind. I'm thankful for friends who had Leuko tape. I wouldn't have made it without this wonderful invention.

This past March, early in the season, the family and I decided to set up at Gooch Gap. Gooch Gap is only seventeen miles from the official starting point of the Appalachian Trail at Springer Mountain. If the thru hikers start at the walkup trail from Amicalola Falls then it's eight additional miles. So hikers will have only hiked about twenty five miles max to Gooch Gap. It seems strange to set up here, but you'd be amazed how happy hikers are to see someone this early on the trail. Often you are the first "trail blessing" they come across in their hike. Additionally, we find this is a great spot to bless people with the foot care kits, because two or three days is about what it takes to figure out if you have the wrong shoes.

This day was a beautiful sunny day, the type that is in short supply in early spring Appalachia. We had several hikers come by and grab fruit, energy bars, chocolate bars, and drinks. One fellow came and stood with us for a while. We love when people hang around, and pepper us with questions. Why were we there? Did we hike? How did the kids like our lifestyle and work? He had previously hiked southbound from Maine and was finishing up a small section of Georgia he had missed due to winter the year before. He turned his attention to our foot care kits and asked who those were for.

"They are for anyone that needs them. We figured we would run into someone in this area that is struggling with their feet."

He knew just the people. He had encountered a group of ladies who were all having issues with their feet. They were a couple miles back at the shelter and were stopping for the day because of their foot pain and blisters. I mentioned I would hike the kits up to the shelter, but he had already taken his pack off and volunteered for the job. We agreed to watch his hiking gear and he took off running up the trail with the foot care kits.

This is a great time to mention that people on trail will literally give you the shirt off their back. Regardless of religious belief, or lifestyle preference, I have seen hikers from every creed and walk of life do selfless acts of beauty to help others. I believe this is part of the reason why hikers have trouble assimilating back to "normal" American living, because you see less of this type of love in "normal" life.

So off our friend goes, running up the trail. He made great time, much better than I would have made. When he returned he told us these hikers were weeping, in pain and thankfulness, at the shelter when he arrived with the supplies to treat their wounds. We had included in the packages some info about Trail Servants, who we are, what we do, and devotional links for them to follow. We were in the right place, at the right time, to be the hands and feet of Jesus

Psalm 37:23 says the Lord directs the steps of the

Godly. We constantly rely on this direction as we prepare to go into the field and minister to the hurting. I've had people ask me how I knew to be in a certain location. How did I know to have exactly the supplies that were needed that day? The answer is I have never known. We simply pray about the day, and depend on the direction of the Lord, and he puts us in the right places, at the right times, for the right people.

I'm always praying for divine appointments. If you are unfamiliar with the term, it's God putting us in the place we need to be, to see the people he desires for us to see. There are over three million people who will set foot on the Appalachian Trail in a given year.[1] You could have hundreds of workers on the trail and not touch every single person who is hiking in a given year, but I trust God will lead me to the ones He has prepared for me to see. He will clearly show us the people He intends for us to help, and I know that nothing happens by chance. It's always His divine appointment.

I hope that each of us understands this principle in our own lives. We miss opportunities to share with and help the hurting and broken because we don't see the divine appointments in our everyday lives. We fail to think about the number of people we interact with, and the potential impact of each interaction. Let's do some math.

On average we live 78 years. Now subtract 5 years for the period of life we have little memory of meeting people. Assume we meet 3 new people per day and there are 365 days in a year. So, (73 x 3) x 365 = 79,935, or basically 80,000 people we will interact with at least once in a given lifetime. We know many we will interact with much more than one time.[2]

We often find ourselves in the right place for the right interaction, but understanding God is giving us opportunities helps us not to waste these moments. We must learn to be very intentional in our interactions. Too often we dismiss things as happy coincidences when they are moments ordained by the Creator Himself. I challenge you to begin each day praying God will set up divine appointments for you, then when you meet people throughout the day you don't lose sight of the potential impact that meeting can have.

Reflection

1. Reflect on a time when God allowed you to be in the right place, at the right time to bless another.
2. Do these moments happen often for you? If not, what can you do to increase your chances of these interactions?
3. Has God ever allowed someone to bless your life at just the right time and place?

LESSON #4
EXPERT ADVICE

"Every man gets a narrower and narrower field of knowledge in which he must be an expert in order to compete
with other people. The specialist knows more and more
about less and less and finally knows everything about
nothing."

— KONRAD LORENZ

Occasionally, I will attempt to pick up a new
hobby. Usually hobbies will include things that
don't tie up too much emotional energy, and
allow me to relax and think. This made fly fishing for trout
the perfect relaxing new hobby. How hard can fly fishing
be? I grew up fishing, and this was an opportunity to enjoy
the mountains near Shady Valley, TN, literally right down
the street.

I quickly learned there is a big difference in fly fishing
and fishing for catfish or crappie in the local south
Alabama body of water. For one, there was a plethora of

different confusing types of tackle. There were big flys, little flies, flies that looked like little fuzzy worms, and flies that were so small I wondered if the fish could see them. Then you had to tie these flies onto your reel. I have fairly good eyesight as long as I've got my glasses or contacts, but trying to figure out how to place these tiny lures onto the line was an adventure itself, but I had a new rod my mom had bought me for Christmas, three small flies, and a little extra line. How hard could this be?

Fly fishing is hard if you have no idea what you're doing. I drove down to Backbone Rock and was pleasantly surprised that I was alone. "Good," I thought. No one was around to witness me trying to get this gear together and figuring this out on my own. Like my initial backpacking excursions, I hadn't reviewed any YouTube videos of how to use my rod, how to tie flies, or techniques associated with the craft. I was going down to the river and learning for myself, I'll never learn.

Sitting on the rock casting my line into the flowing water of Beaverdam Creek made me feel like a real trout fisherman. I had seen the movie, *A River Runs Through It*, and my line swung back and forth the way their line did in the movie. "At least I looked really cool," I thought. Yep, I wasn't catching anything, because I didn't have a clue what I was doing, but I was going to look good doing it. Then I noticed I had some company.

A black Jeep had pulled up across the road driven by a fellow who REALLY looked like he knew what he was doing. I observed him as he opened the back hatch and started thumbing through his equipment. I had determined if someone arrived who looked like they knew what they were doing, and seemed pretty chill, I would ask for some advice. I pulled what little gear I had together and jogged across the road to meet my new friend. He saw me coming and asked if the fish were biting. I laughed to myself knowing my answer wouldn't help him.

"I'm really not sure, I have no clue what I'm doing, I'm a newbie," I answered.

"Well, I'm a trout fishing guide, just out fishing a little for myself today, but I'd love to show you what I know," he responded.

I couldn't believe my luck. I was a novice who had ran into an expert willing to share his knowledge. He walked over to my truck to check out my rod. Wouldn't you know it. I didn't have the right fly for the conditions, and didn't have the fly tied correctly. He showed me the technique and set up the rod properly. Who knew you could tie both a topwater and sinker fly onto the same tippet? An expert; that's who. My first lesson was the most important for a guy who grew up fishing with a regular fishing rod. In fly fishing you cast the line, not the fly. The fly goes where the line goes. In bass fishing you cast the lure, but flies are too small so you must depend on the line in trout fishing. Then we went over to the river and he began to go through the lay of the river. First, you need to see where the river runs, and where it sits flat. The trout like to sit in the flat water where they spend fewer calories fighting the current, and let the river bring the flies down to them like a conveyor belt. So, you can cast into the current and let the bait flow back into the flat water. Or, you can see the ledges where the water is darker and deeper; fish like to sit on these underwater overhangs. Cast with the current and let it pull you through these areas. You can also cast against the current and strip the line back through the current to catch fish being pushed along by the river's flow. I'd been fishing for over an hour and hadn't seen a fish. After twenty minutes with this fellow, we had two good size trout in the bag.

What type of trout are in Tennessee? I get this question anytime I mention fishing in the mountains. I admit, I thought trout were trout until I started fishing with my new friend. I learned there are three types of trout in east Tennessee. These include Brook trout, Rainbow trout, and Brown trout. Brook trout are the native species in Tennessee, with Rainbow and Brown trout being imported by the Tennessee Wildlife Resources Agency. Basically, they stock the rivers and streams throughout the year with smaller trout. If you are catching large trout you are normally catching holdovers from previous years' stock. Who knew? The expert knew; that's who. Finally, I asked a question I was sure would stump my new friend. Even an expert might have trouble with this question; I sure didn't understand it.

"How do you know when to use which fly?"

My buddy had hundreds of flies, all shapes and sizes. I had exactly three flies. When do you use the topwater, the larva, the sinker, the fuzzy worm, the colorful ones, and dull ones? This was the question of questions, it had me stumped. So, do you want to know what his answer was? It's so simple, so simple I was kind of embarrassed I asked the question.

"You watch the river, see what the fish seem to be hitting, what type flies are hatching and on the water, and that's what you cast."

Such a simple answer, and there can be more to it depending on the time of year, but basically you watch the fish. You see, experts have a way of understanding what seems complex, and explaining it in a way that is understandable. Wow, we can learn a lot from people who have gone before us and have all this knowledge.

This is the lesson here; we all need people in our lives who can help us learn and grow. We all need mentors. I learned more in two hours fishing with an expert than most people learn about trout in a year on their own. Often we struggle with trial and error in life when in reality we could simply find someone we trust, who has been down that road already, and ask them to pour their knowledge into our life. Expert advice helps us gain knowledge much quicker than trial and error.

Proverbs 11:14 tells us, "Where there is no guidance, a people falls, but in an abundance of counselors there is safety." Kings and leaders have depended on trusted advice of counselors for centuries. King Soloman, the wisest man who has ever lived, said, "there is safety in having those around you who can speak wisdom into your life." Why do we think we can get by living on an island with no expert advice?

We see mentorship in both the Old and New testaments. Jesus spent three years teaching his disciples, Paul had a steady stream of mentees throughout his time serving the Lord, and these disciples went on to make more disciples. It is my prayer that you find a Godly mentor, learn everything you can, and apply those lessons to your life. If you are older, and already established, seek out those younger who are looking for wisdom and pour everything you know into them.

Again, King Soloman writes in Proverbs 27:17, "Iron sharpens iron, and one man sharpens another." We are better when we have counsel and advice from trusted mentors. I will use this space for a word of caution. As one sharpens another, they can also dull another. I'm sad to say I've known some who have chosen the wrong people to influence their lives; people who seem to be upstanding but have led them away from proper Biblical teaching, and ultimately dulled their Christian walk. So, the questions are, "What makes a good mentor?" and "How do we find trusted mentors?"

We can't all just have an expert pull up alongside us like I had with my fishing guide. Sometimes it takes a little work to find the expert advice of a mentor, but I'll give you my best advice on how to identify individuals who could be of help to you. Primarily, I believe mentors must be encouragers. I put this skill alongside the other primary trait which is subject knowledge. A good mentor must be skilled in your area of interest, and they must be an encouragement. I have some good mentors, and when I hang up the phone or get off video chat, I always feel like I can run through a wall. I feel nothing is impossible, and I'm filled with faith.

A mentor needs to have the proper life experience. Note, I am not saying they have to be old, they just need to have some experience under their belt. Too often we equate age with maturity and experience. This is not always the case. Also, we see knowledge as experience. This is not always the case. I mentioned a mentor must be knowledgeable, they must also have experience. I know lots of people with knowledge, but no real world experience. Some people know everything about hiking gear, but they've never been on a trail. There is some knowledge that only comes from experience. Seek mentors with both.

Trust is a factor, both in a mentor and in finding a mentor. Mentors must be individuals you can trust. Can you trust what they tell you? Can you trust they've got your best interest in mind? Can you trust they are giving good, Godly advice? If the answer is yes, then proceed. In finding a mentor the one option is asking a trusted source, who they might recommend.

While some mentors are assigned, as in college, I prefer an old fashioned approach. I still believe the best option is praying and asking God to reveal who should be allowed to speak into your life, and make a way for that relationship to form naturally. Regardless, understand that mentorship is entirely Biblical.

<u>Reflection</u>

1. What are qualities that make a great mentor?
2. Reflect on a time when someone took you under their wing and helped you succeed. Why do good mentors add value and help create success?
3. Where can you find an opportunity for you to mentor another?

LESSON #5
WE MAKE THIS LOOK EASY

"Don't be fooled, people are not who the "post" to be."

— UNKNOWN

I have a hiker friend who says he believes we do a disservice to people because we often make hiking look too appealing online. Let me illustrate this for you. Almost every hiker we meet has an Instagram account. These accounts are full of sweeping vistas, mountain overlooks, smiles from mountaintop views, and juicy burgers served by a Trail Angel like myself. If the total hike takes one hundred fifty days, you will see about fifty days worth of pictures, full of just the most beautiful and appealing parts of the journey. What about those other hundred days?

Those other hundred days are filled with cold mornings, frozen socks, biting insects, sprained ankles, swollen knees, near dehydration, and restless nights. These are just a small part of the things you don't see. What we see is the highlight reel, the cherry picked best days, the one beautiful photo in the middle of the worst week ever. However, because what we see becomes the reality we know, we assume the whole hike was a great time, full of good food and few troubles. That's simply never the case.

We do this in our lives off trail as well. We post pictures of the new car, the birthday dinner, the kids' baptism, the clean house, and the concerts. We wouldn't dare let anyone think our lives were anything less than perfect. I get it, I do the same and there is nothing wrong with it. The problem comes with comparison.

So often we compare ourselves to the lives of others. We compare our journey to the journey of others. The problem is we know everything about our lives. We know the bad and the problematic. We know we can't afford that car, that our kids fight on the way to church, that the house is rarely clean; that we have issues. Then, we see these perfect lives we perceive the rest of the world to have, and we feel defeated, broken. We compare their highlight reel to our complete game.

Theodore Roosevelt once said, "Comparison is the thief of joy." Such true words! When we make these comparisons it makes us question our own self worth. We believe everyone else somehow got to take the easy road in life while we are stuck on the hard path. What did I do to deserve the hand I've been given? Don't fall into this trap!

Hikers quickly realize the fallacy of the perfect days, perfect weather, and easy miles. Those social media pictures were very nice, but there are many hard miles in between those waterfalls and ponies. Sometimes people become discouraged; some quit and go home.

Likewise, I feel there is a correlation between the high

incidences of anxiety and depression reported, and the time we spend looking at the "perfect" lives of everyone on social media. We feel our lives aren't as glamorous as the next guy. We become envious of those perfect smiles and shiny things. In reality, it's all a facade, and mentally it's destroying us. So, for the sake of helping us all, I'd like to offer a few tidbits of knowledge.

First, understand that most of what you see on social media is an illusion. You see the mountaintop vista, but you don't realize there is a road nearby and the photographer drives to the spot. It looks like they hiked up and didn't break a sweat, but it's an illusion. You see the new Tahoe pulling the boat to the lake, but you don't see the strain of debt and working sixteen hour days. You see the singer in the video with the jewelry, the cars, and the house. What you don't realize is it's all rented and nothing is real.

Second, life just isn't always fair. This is a fact of life. I never ran a 4.4 second forty yard dash and was never going to play football in the Southeastern Conference. We all have different talents, but if you constantly tribulate over what you can't do, over the unfairness of life, you will never be who God created you to be. Focus on your strengths, train your strengths, rely on the Lord's strength; life was never supposed to be fair.

I had to learn this last point the hard way as a young minister. It's simply this, you must be who you are. You will never find true freedom until you understand nobody can be a better you than you, and you will constantly feel depressed trying to be someone else. I read lots of classic sermons, and tried to sound like those great men of God. I tried to set my sermons up like Spurgeon, and use my country accent like Billy Graham. It didn't work. It was never going to work. Finally, I just decided to be me. Sometimes humorous, sometimes loud, sometimes three points, sometimes five. I just had to be me, and you just have to be you. God created you with unique personality traits, unique style, unique attitude. Be who he created you to be.

I'm reminded of a passage from the 21st chapter of the Gospel of John. Jesus is speaking to Peter, asking Peter three times to reaffirm his love for Him. Jesus then gave Peter a glimpse of the fate that would eventually await him in death, telling Peter he would stretch out his hands, and others would dress him and take him where he would not want to go. Peter sees John and immediately asks a question to compare their fate. Peter says, "What about him?" Jesus replied "If I want him to remain alive until I return, what is that to you? As for you, follow me." [1]

Is it fair John would be the only disciple to die a natural death? Is it fair that John's brother would be the first to die just a short time later? Jesus quickly put Peter's attempt at comparison to bed, and simply said, "you follow me." Don't worry about the other guy, that's not for you to know. For many of us we need to take this lesson to heart. I think Jesus would tell each of us, don't worry about the Jones', you follow me.

<u>**Reflection**</u>

1. How do you feel comparison affects your life on a day to day basis?
2. I listed a few tidbits of information to help limit the effects of comparison. List more helpful ideas that help defeat comparison.
3. There are several verses in scripture that deal with comparison. Use your available tools (concordance, study Bible, Google) and decide which of these is most impactful for you and write your thoughts below.

LESSON #6

BAIT

Watch and pray so that you will not fall into temptation.
The spirit is willing, but the body is weak.

— MATTHEW 26:41

I'm going to venture back to our previous lesson on
fly fishing. Let's go a little more in depth on the
subject of bait. One difference in fishing lakes back
home and fly fishing was the type of bait used. The flies
are smaller, and much lighter than traditional bass fishing
lures I was accustomed to casting. Due to their light-
weight design you can't simply cast a fly and have its
weight propel the line forward; you must cast the line and
the fly follows the line. This is where the beautiful snap-
ping of the fly line comes into play. Those big circular
motions with the line whipping around over the fisherman's head. It's a thing of beauty, but also a necessity. You
have to build up the momentum of the line to cast the fly.

One way to understand the types of flies is to understand the life cycle of insects. Everything about fly fishing is made to mimic the insects trout normally feed upon. There are four stages of an insect's life. The Nymph stage is where insects sit on the river bottom and bounce along with the current. The Emerger stage is when they start to get to topwater and are developing wings. In the Adult stage insects fly around and occasionally land on the water. Finally, the Spinner stage is where insects are later in life and just lay around on the water.[1]

These life cycles lead to the beautifully tied flies trout fisherman use. There are flies that sink, flies that float, and flies that hover in the mid-range between the bottom and the top. Fishermen will tell you observing the trout and seeing what they're hitting at that time of year is key. If you can figure out what they're eating then your ability to entice the fish will increase.

When I started fly fishing I had maybe five flies total. I thought that was awesome. I could lose four of these things and still be able to fish. I quickly found out the arsenal of a trout fisherman was many more than five lures. Some people have so many lures they arrange them by type: dry or wet. Dry stays on top of the water, wet sinks. Then they arrange them by colors or patterns. A good fly fisherman might have hundreds of lures on any given fishing trip. This is all done to present the most tempting option to the fish. You have to use bait that will catch their eye and entice them to hit the fly.

Obviously this lesson isn't about fly fishing bait. Perhaps you can see where we're going with this. Every person that has ever lived has experienced temptation. We have been baited by the enemy, who is a careful observer, an enemy who knows what to present and when to present the bait.

The key to bait is catching the eye of the fish. The fish is enticed, drawn away from the safety of the rock shelf. This sounds an awful lot like James 1:13-15. James says each person is tempted, drawn away by his desires and enticed. Every day marriages, relationships, families, and churches are torn apart because individuals give into temptation.

Hand in hand with catching the eye of the fish is timing. A good fisherman knows exactly the perfect time of day to fish. Seasons change this timing, but a good fisherman will get up early or stay out late to find the perfect time to cast the bait.

This is how Satan, the enemy, lays the trap for us as well. It's all about timing. In an earlier chapter I mention when the wrong time, and the wrong opportunity cross paths that can lead to destruction. We have a big part to play in this area of temptation. If we know there are certain times and places where we are tempted, then we can't let ourselves get into those situations.

When I straightened up and chose to follow hard after God in my early twenties, I still had to be very careful. Two things I couldn't do for those first couple years. I couldn't go to a tailgate at a college football event, and I had to minimally grill out. This was because my mind correlated drinking so heavily with tailgates and cookouts. I knew it would be a tempting encounter for me to partici-pate in either of those activities at this time, so I stayed completely away from them. Today, I can sit at a tailgate. The friendly folks at the tent next door may offer me whiskey; remember, they don't know me, and I can politely turn it down. I now cook out all the time. I cook for hikers, at times grilling several days per week. I'm more mature now in my walk; I'm not tempted in these situations. I get offered drugs and alcohol many times over the course of a hiking season, usually from people new to me. They don't know I'm a missionary yet. I like to make the comment, "My occupation frowns on it," when the offer comes. Without fail someone will ask, "What do you do, Shep?" I reply, "I'm a Chaplain to hikers." Then the unsuspecting person will straighten themselves up appalled and say something like, "I can't believe I just offered drugs to a preacher." I assure them I'm not offended. Actually, I've realized it is special for someone to offer you something of value that is hard to come by in the woods. Believe it or not, the person making the offer is being extremely gracious and generous.

When I was a youth pastor, I always told my youth they had to be careful about the situations they put themselves in. The best way to avoid temptation is never let yourself get into a tempting place. Maybe they were tempted to look at bad things on the computer after everyone else went to sleep. So, make sure you go to sleep before everyone else. Or, you're tempted by the television in your bedroom, get rid of the TV. I had to be careful how I preached this, because I ended up with a smashed laptop computer and a power cord cut clean from the back of the TV on my desk once. I told them to make sure their parents knew I did not tell them to destroy their stuff, but I was thrilled they took it so seriously. The Bible takes this seriously as well. Matthew 5:30 says, "If your right hand causes you to sin, cut it off. If your eye offends you, pluck it out." Let's get real about this stuff.

No one is immune from temptation. Anyone who says

otherwise is a liar. Temptation in itself is not sinful. I remember when I was a young believer I'd have a thought race through my head. I wouldn't dwell on it, but I still felt I'd done something wrong. This led to a constant internal struggle. Finally, I realized a fleeting thought, an unintended glance, wasn't sin. The enemy was just keeping me distracted with these internal dilemmas. Sinful thoughts are the ones you dwell on, the ones that take you deeper into sinful actions, which the Bible tells us will eventually lead to destruction. So, how do we "beat the bait?"

First, the Word says in 2 Corinthians 10:3-5 to take every thought captive to obey Christ. This is a very "churchy" phrase, I'm aware. For me this means immediately meeting intrusive thoughts with scripture, and with the name of Jesus. I have a couple friends the Lord got hold of around the same time as me. We would get together and discuss this, and finally we determined any time an intrusive thought came into our minds, we'd immediately utter the phrase, "In the name of Jesus get away from me." We'd just rebuke the thought quickly. I'm sure we looked crazy in those early days walking through the mall silently muttering that phrase, but I'm just being real and telling you what worked for me. When Jesus was tempted He immediately met those temptations with scripture.

You can't fight thoughts with thoughts. The enemy will simply outsmart you. You must be able to fight temptation with scripture. If it worked for Jesus, it should work for us. Perhaps you don't have the perfect scripture for what you're facing; just quote what you know. If all you have is John 3:16, then quote it first, then go and learn more scripture. I purposely learned scripture in the beginning that dealt with my struggles; I knew I would need it. You have to prepare yourself to fight for what you need.

Preparation is key to temptation. The worst time to start learning to fight is in the fight. The best time is before the fight. I call it "prepare over repair." Some endurance athletes say, "be hard when it gets hard." You've prayed, studied, and learned scripture, so now you're ready when the enemy casts the bait in front of you.

The enemy of your soul comes to steal, kill, and destroy. Our job is to make ourselves the hardest target we can. James tells us, "Resist the devil and he will flee." Eventually the tempter leaves for a season. He goes off to find an easier victim. I always note, even with Jesus it says he left, "for a season." He's coming back, you'll be tempted again, but you'll be battle hardened and prepared for the fight.

<u>Reflection</u>

1. Can you identify situations that you know offer more temptations in your life? If so, how can you keep yourself from these situations in advance?
2. Why does the devil use different bait for different people? Are we tempted to see our temptations as smaller, insignificant, and other peoples as large and dangerous?
3. How are you preparing today for the temptations of tomorrow?

LESSON #7
COOKS VS. CHEFS

"Very few people are original. There's very little original anything out there. Because to be original means you have to stand alone."

— SUSAN POWTER

In my work, as a Chaplain to hikers and outdoor enthusiasts, I have the good pleasure of meeting all sorts of people. Without a doubt I meet quite a few originals. People who chose to look at life from a different angle, those who refuse to follow the well worn path or take the beaten trail. Some literally develop trails of their own.

I met Jason, known on trail as Out and About, while hiking in Florida in 2022. We got along very well, and became fast friends in the muddy knee deep water that shaped the week I spent with his hiking family. After the Florida Trail, he decided to hit the Pinhoti Trail, and offered for me to tag along. As we walked I peppered him with questions about his plans for the rest of the year, and was surprised to hear him talking about a new route he was planning to hike. I mean, is there anything new in 2022? He planned to take the Mountain to Sea Trail, link it with the Palmetto Trail back to the Benton Mackaye Trail, and with an added road walk have a loop called the Carolinian. This 2,200 mile loop would take him through the states of NC, SC, TN, and GA. The trails were already there, but the loop had never been put together; he was doing it first. He had the vision to see what was there and create something new. You see, my friend Jason is a chef.

Chef's don't look up recipes in a cookbook, they create recipes that cooks follow. Chefs challenge the status quo; they are the ones who change the landscape around them. Chef's are world changers. To be a chef it takes courage, the kind of courage most modern schools squeeze out of you. Truth be told, many churches squeeze it out of you as well. We are taught to follow all the prescribed rules, look just alike, and act just alike. We become so transfixed on our customs, habits and traditions, we miss opportunities to stand out, be creative, different, and special.

I've always been a little unusual. After fifteen plus years as a minister I could write a book on how NOT to do ministry. Some of my more unorthodox ideas included middle of the night prayer sessions with youth, taking all the chairs out of the youth room and just sitting on the floor, walking across Alabama, riding a lawn mower in a field and letting people pay to shoot paintballs at me as a fundraiser; the list is long. Here's the deal, I still have people who come up to me and remember those times.

"Remember when Pastor Brad took all the chairs away? I thought it was cool to just sit on the floor."

"I'll never forget throwing frozen turkeys at Thanksgiving for prizes, or playing capture the flag until 1am."

These are some of the reasons I love youth pastors. Sometimes we've all gone too far with an idea, but these guys can come up with the craziest ideas. I love their energy. These young guns are usually chefs, and I hate to see us try to turn them into cooks. When I retire from missions I'm going back to be a youth pastor. I'm going to play glow in the dark volleyball at 65.

Chefs cook from scratch, they don't use the box. Your whole life you've been in a box. You are born and put in a box. We grow up in a box, then go to school in a big brick box. We go to church in a box. We drive to church in a box. We go to work and guess where we are, in a box. Honestly, the American dream, a little white house, a picket fence, 2.5 kids and a golden retriever, is a neat little box.

Truth be told I've always been a little outside the box. It's really no surprise the Lord would call me into a ministry that is so far outside the box of normal Christian ministry. As God prepared me to minister outside the normal box one story stands out.

Once, when I was a Pastor I needed to visit a congregant who was in the Intensive Care Unit. Michelle waited in the car and I went up to visit, I told her I'd be back in about ten minutes. I got to the waiting area and took a seat, it was almost time to go in. Suddenly, this man sitting down from me said, "We need to pray for our loved ones before we go in, and I think this man here should lead the prayer." He was pointing at me. So, I got up and prayed with all the family members in the ICU waiting room. Good story, right?

Then a lady came over to me. She explained that she was there to see her sister, Her sister was a new Christian, but she was dying. She had never had a chance to get in church or be baptized since she accepted Christ as her Savior. She asked if I'd go with her to visit her sister.

We entered the ICU unit, and I followed the dying lady's sister into her room. She was hooked up to tons of wires and had a tube keeping her from speaking, but she was awake and could nod her head. I told her I was a minister. I met her sister and came to see her. She nodded that she knew Christ as Savior. I felt I should ask her if she wanted to be baptized, but obviously she couldn't be baptized, she was immobile. I couldn't shake the feeling so I asked, "Would you like to be baptized?" She nodded, yes. Her sister looked at me excitedly and asked if I was for real. She said it would mean so much. I told the dying woman baptism is an outward symbol of the inward decision. It didn't save us and we wouldn't be able to do it full immersion, but God saw her heart in the matter. He saw she wanted to be obedient.

I had her sister go get a large cup from the nurses center. I noticed all the ICU nurses craning their heads around to see what was happening. I took the cup, filled it with water, and gave it to her sister. I cupped my hands over the head of the sick woman, and had her sister pour water into my hands. Then, I spoke the words of Baptism, and released the water from my hands over the head of the dying woman. Tears rolled from her eyes and she raised one hand in worship. What a moment. I got back to my car 40 minutes later. Michelle was shocked when I explained the reason I ran late was due to baptizing a lady in the ICU.

I want you to repeat after me, CREATIVITY IS NOT A SIN. Okay! Let's try another one. DOING IT DIFFERENTLY THAN YOU'VE ALWAYS DONE IT IS NOT A SIN. Look at you!

I'm not the most creative person by nature. I listen to the Holy Spirit, who I believe is extremely creative, and I surround myself with creative people. Let's consider God's creativity.

In Joshua 6 we learn of the siege at Jericho. In ancient times, when a city was besieged, the army outside would set up camp and wait out the people inside. Effectively starving those unfortunate souls trapped inside, and eventually they became overwhelmed by disease and starvation. The catch is that occasionally help would arrive if the inhabitants inside the city could hold on. Or, some internal strife might arise that compelled the attackers outside to give up the siege. This was the normal way, the recipe for a siege, the way cooks throughout the ages had done it. But God called Joshua aside and here is what he said, "Every day for six days walk around the city once with all the men of war. Then, on the seventh day walk around the city seven times, and have the priests blow the trumpets. The walls will fall down flat, and I will deliver the enemy to you."

Say what, God? Never, never has it ever been done like that. That's not in any of the siege textbooks, no army does it that way. That is definitely not the recipe. You see, the Holy Spirit is looking for chefs willing to follow Him into places we've never been. People who are obedient, willing to look foolish. Let's consider David.

1st Samuel introduces us to a young shepherd boy named David. We know the story but I'll run it down for you. The Philistines brought their army out to battle against the Israelites. David's brothers went out to fight, and his father sent him later with provisions for his brothers. Young David hears the giant, Goliath, roar; he hears him curse God and mock the Isrealites, and he refuses to stand for it. He volunteers to fight. What does Saul do? He goes to the recipe book and breaks out his armor for the boy, because that's how you're supposed to fight. You take your helmet, your sword, your coat of mail, and you go fight. That's the plan; that's the blueprint.

You see, David was a chef, not just any chef, an anointed chef. He had already been visited by Samuel, and had oil poured over his head. When you're walking in the anointing of God, creativity to overcome obstacles comes naturally. So, what does David do? He takes his sling, five stones and his confidence in the Lord, and destroys the Philistine champion. Not one soul who watched this display had ever seen a champion with a sword and spear lose to a shepherd's sling. David was a chef.

When I left my job and my boss told me, "they're not going to believe you're leaving to be a missionary on the Appalachian Trail," I didn't realize it then, but God was calling me to be a chef. I am not alone in this call. I believe many of you reading these words have calls on your life. Calls to launch out into unchartered waters; calls to serve in unusual places. Or perhaps, to minister in a usual place in a slightly different way than you've ever done it. The creativity of the Holy Spirit is bold, and available if we stop to listen and obey.

<u>Reflection</u>

1. Can you think of any modern day chefs or people who challenged the status quo? What were their contributions? Would their contributions have been different if they had chosen the normal path?
2. I believe God uses us supernaturally in things we are naturally inclined to do. What are some areas you enjoy? (Perhaps rodeo, dance, fishing tournaments, video games, camping, etc.)
3. Have you ever felt God calling you to step outside the box? Perhaps becoming a chef in an area of our natural inclinations we mentioned above?

LESSON #8
WHEREVER HE LEADS

"I don't think that we're meant to understand it all the time. I think that sometimes we just have to have faith."

— NICHOLAS SPARKS

As some of you know, I'm not the most handy fellow. I have lots of skills, just not many translate into building and home repair. I learned long ago that if you don't have the skills you better find someone that has those skills you need, and get them on your team. Thankfully, my brother Derek, known near and far as Pug, is exceptionally talented at carpentry, electrical, and general handy work.

It was last April and we were working full steam to get the lot in Shady Valley up and running. Pug decided to come up, and we would handle some of the projects left over from the previous year. He also brought along his dog Rufus. Ole Rufus is a pretty good dog. He's a Blue Heeler, and those type dogs really love the mountains and

Appalachian Trail. This dog followed Pug everywhere he went, just wanting to be near his master.

Upon arriving at the lot I noticed it was a good bit cooler than I expected, perhaps cooler than we had packed clothes for. We drove down to the local Dollar General and I took note of the low gray clouds. I knew from experience what these meant. You couldn't see the mountains on the other side of the valley because of these low, gray behemoths. I asked Pug if he'd brought clothes for snowy weather. He quickly replied, "I'm not planning on being in snowy weather." Here's the thing about Pug, he gets cold very easily; he hates the cold about as much as my wife. As we went into the store the attendant yelled a greeting and said, "You boys getting ready for the snow?"

Pug was not happy that my observation about potential snow was correct. He went through grabbing extra blankets, socks, and anything he thought would help the situation. I grabbed some cookies and milk. That's the kind of layer I like to put on to stay warm. We gathered our dollar store loot and headed for the camper. Yes, we still live in the mountains in a sixteen foot camper, but by the grace of the Lord we will soon build a small cabin to have more congenial accommodations.

We arrived at the camper, grabbed Rufus from his carrier, and sprinted for the door. It was cold and snow was starting to blow sideways. This isn't that little dainty snowflake snow like we see on television. Imagine someone throwing Nerds candy at you as hard as they can throw it. Or, Dippin Dots when they first come out of the freezer. This snow is stinging pellets. Pug and I jumped into the camper and got the lights on. I was about to shut us in for the night when I noticed ole Rufus just standing outside the door. He refused to come into the camper. Pug called him and clapped his hands. Nothing. Rufus just stood out there in the cold blowing snow. Finally, Pug had to go back outside and physically move Rufus inside the camper.

My first thought was, "How crazy is this dog?" He'd walk all over this property following after his master, and then refuse to come into a perfectly good safe place. A place his owner was calling him into. A place of warmth from the elements. Safety from the cold. Why would he be so obstinate?

My second thought was the hard rebuke that comes from the Holy Spirit, and hits me between the eyes. That shot you don't see coming. The Holy Spirit is really good at nailing me like that. God said, "You know sometimes you're just like ole Rufus. You follow me and know I'm good. You say you'll follow me anywhere, in any situation. Then, I ask you to do something different, something you're not as comfortable with, and you freeze. You'll stand looking at the provision of God right in front of you and not move because you're afraid." Whew! Like I said, sometimes that uppercut from the Holy Spirit comes out of nowhere and hits hard.

I'm reminded of a song we sang in church growing up. Usually it was the benediction, the song sang right before we dismissed. The song is entitled, "Wherever He Leads I'll Go." Many people know the song, few people know the writer, and nobody really remembers the story behind the song.

Baylus Benjamin (B.B.) McKinney was a songwriter and worked for the Southern Baptist Convention. One evening he sat for dinner with a missionary friend, R.S. Jones.

Mr. Jones had served many years as a missionary in Brazil, but doctors had advised him not to return due to recent sickness. B.B. McKinney wondered aloud how his friend would move forward. What will you do after working in South America all these years? What is your plan? Are you worried about the future? Mr. Jones answered, "I don't know, but wherever He leads I'll go." It was the words of his missionary friend that led B.B. McKinney to pen the now beloved hymn. [1]

So, here's the question, "Are we prepared to follow the Lord wherever He leads?" The old adage is sometimes true, "We don't tell lies, we go to church and sing them." We loudly sing that we will follow, and when the time comes to take the step, we freeze. Ole Rufus was more than willing to follow Derek to the shed, to the stream, to the truck, but when it came time to step into the camper, the unknown, he froze. Even though everything he needed was inside the warm camper, he refused.

We have to learn to trust the leading of the Lord. To follow Him even if we are fearful. Look to the six promises the Lord makes to direct our steps found in Psalms and Proverbs. . .

1. Psalm 37:23-24 (NKJV) "The steps of a good man are ordered by the Lord, and he delights in his way. Though he fall, he shall not be utterly cast down."

2. Proverbs 16:9 (NKJV) "A man's heart plans his way, but the Lord directs his steps"

3. Psalms 31:14-15 (NKJV) "But as for me, I trust in you, O Lord; I say, "You are my God." My times are in your hand; deliver me from the

hands of my enemies, and from those who persecute me."

4. Proverbs 20:24 (NKJV) "A man's steps are of the Lord; how then can a man understand his own way?"

5. Psalms 119:105 (NKJV) "Your word is a lamp to my feet and a light to my path."

6. Proverbs 19:21 (NKJV) "There are many plans in a man's heart, nevertheless the Lord's counsel- that will stand."

So, we see our steps are ordered, directed, trusted, understood, enlightened, and on firm foundation when we trust in the Lord.

<u>Reflection</u>

1. Why is it important to follow wherever the Lord leads?
2. Do you make decisions based on comfort, predictability and fear, or faith?
3. Has there ever been a time when God called you to follow Him outside of your comfort zone? Describe the situation.

LESSON # 9
PROGRESS

"Don't compare your progress to that of others. We need our own time to travel our own distance."

— ANONYMOUS

Progress is a funny thing. Mark Twain said, "The secret to progress is to get started." As I write this we are approaching March, which is the traditional starting month for many aspiring Appalachian Trail thru-hikers. These hikers will take their first steps off Springer Mountain and begin a journey of 2200 miles. The young, fittest of the bunch will be done by July, having averaged nearly 25 miles per day over the trip. It's hard for me to imagine hiking a marathon per day for three months, but it happens every year. The motivated souls pressing to get to another long trail and perhaps complete all three major American long trails in a year. I know a lot of these folks; I feed them, minister to them, but rarely hike very long with them for obvious reasons. The majority of hikers progress a little slower down the trail, and these are my hiking partners.

For the majority, the Appalachian Trail is not a three month journey, but a six month journey. Averaging maybe 8 miles per day in north Georgia, and progressing to 18-20 mile days in Virginia. Here we find the hikers forty-one year old Shep will jump in with. This group will finish in October, just short of the late season deadline and closure of Mt. Katahdin.

I tip my hat to the motivated, fast paced few. However, we all know that each person is different, so we move at a separate pace. The key is progress. Slow progress is still progress. Slow progress beats no progress. This is true if we are hiking a long trail, losing weight, getting back into educational endeavors, or rebuilding relationships with our kids. Everyone may have the same goal, but it's unrealistic to think everyone will have the same pace.

I ran a marathon once. I know, I know, it's hard to believe, but it happened. I remember getting to the starting line and seeing these people holding up cards with different times on them. One said 2:30, another read 4:00, and another 5:00. They explained these were pacers. People who had run many marathons and excelled at keeping you at a certain pace. If you wanted to finish in four hours you got in the group with the lady holding the 4:00. I believe I started with the 4:30 group, and ran with this group until the halfway mark. At that point I developed intense foot pain and had to slow down, but I kept moving forward. Eventually, I fell in with a slower pace group. I finished very near the end. The key is I finished. I'd accomplished a goal. Done something less than .05% of the United States population has ever done. You just have to find your pace and move forward.

While we're on the subject of marathons let me add another thought. I mentioned my painful foot injury caused me to change pace. It makes me think about Isaiah 40:31 when it says "They that wait on the Lord to renew their strength will RUN and not grow weary, WALK and not faint." When things were going good in the marathon I ran, when pain set in, I walked, but I never stopped progressing toward the goal. In your life, run on the good days, walk on the bad days, but never stop moving forward.

If you don't know this yet, hiking a mountain is not a straight up, straight down walk. It's a little up, a little down, back up, over a rock, down a hill, back up and around a bend, then up some more. It's not a straight line-it's non-linear. There are many peaks, valleys, and plateaus involved in progress.

We tend to overestimate what we can do in a day, and underestimate what we can do in a year. We all feel we are moving slow in the present, but don't realize what even slow progress means over time. What if I asked you if you could read 20 books in a year? Most people would balk at that idea. I'd hear things like, "I just don't have the time." Or, "I've never been much of a reader." Ok, so what if I asked you to read just 15 minutes per day? Most would say they could do that, maybe even proudly proclaim they could do 30 minutes. Did you know reading 15 minutes a day will equal, on average, 20 books per year? If you read 30 minutes you'd double it to 40 books. We overestimate the present, and underestimate the future. Have an ultimate goal, and a current goal.

Another key to progress is breaking down your goals into smaller bites. When I said read 20 books you thought that sounded high. When I mentioned reading 15 minutes per day that sounded doable. When I hike I break the walk down. A 100 mile section hike sounds like a long week. Thinking in terms of 15 miles per day sounds better, and 7.5 miles before lunch is great. Then on long climbs I look up and find a point on the mountain, a tree or rock. I hike hard to that tree and take a break. Then I find the next waypoint and start hiking again. I break it down into small, very manageable portions. When you focus on losing forty pounds, that two pound weight loss seems small. When you break it down to ten pounds per month, that two pound loss is 20% of the monthly goal; that's amazing! Progress is about perspective. If you perceive you're making little progress, you're likely to quit. If you perceive you're making slow, steady progress you will continue.

It really is about taking it one day at a time. I've recently gotten into the habit of grading myself daily. I basically have three categories I judge daily: spiritual, mental, and physical. Nothing fancy, just thinking over it at night and grading myself A, B, C, D, F on each of the categories. Spiritually, was God at the center of my decisions today, did I spend time with the Lord, was I sensitive to the Holy Spirit, did I miss opportunities to minister? Mentally, was I emotionally healthy today, or did I get angry and fly off the handle - quick fact - this was a problem for me in times past. I put healthy relationships with my wife and kids into the category as well. Physically, did I move my body, get some exercise, and eat healthier? Did I work on keeping blood pressure low? Doing this daily is just my way of making small improvements every day and this equals major improvements over time. It's just one consistent day at a time. You see how this all fits together? The key is consistency.

Here's another key to progress. Go easy on yourself. If you are making progress, then praise the Lord. It beats the alternative. Sure, you might not go as fast as some, do not beat yourself up. The term here is self-compassion. So what if I'm hiking 15 miles per day and not 25 miles, I'm still on the path, seeing the beauty, probably stopping to smell the roses and enjoy it more. So what if your husband loses 20 pounds in the time it takes you to lose 5 pounds-my wife hates how that works. You're still making progress and getting healthy.

I remember as a younger youth pastor I always got down on myself when camp season rolled around. Some of this goes back to the previous lesson in comparison, but is also relevant here. I would beat myself up on the back of perceived inadequacy when I looked at other groups. I have always struggled with comparison and lack of self-compassion. Maybe that's why these topics made the book, they're hard lessons I've had to learn. DO NOT BEAT YOURSELF UP IF YOU ARE HEADING IN THE RIGHT DIRECTION FAITHFULLY.

Passion means more to progress than perfection ever will. I tell people God does not expect perfection, but he appreciates passion. A good, passionate attitude will keep someone moving forward on the trail, and it will keep you moving forward in life. It's cliche but your attitude does influence your altitude. A bad attitude, failure to appreciate the beauty of the journey, has ended more long distance hikes than bad knees ever will. Remember, bad attitudes hinder progress.

Earlier I mentioned hiking is non-linear. It's ups and downs, highs and lows, but the goal is moving forward. I sat down recently with a hiker who was struggling with these ups and downs. We looked at the story of Elijah in 1 Kings chapters 18 and 19. I explained the mighty victory God won using Elijah on Mt. Carmel in chapter 18. That's a high moment; God was definitely with him in that moment. Then we looked at chapter 19 when Jezebel threatened his life. The prophet runs into the wilderness, sits under a tree, and prays that he might die. He literally said, "I've had enough Lord." Has anyone ever been in that situation? Where you throw your hands into the air and say, "I've had enough Lord!" The ups and downs, plateaus and bends of life. What does the Lord do for the prophet in this low estate? He sends an angel to touch him, feed him, and give him water. Even in the low moments God was with him, sustaining him, and you know he'll do it for you too. Commit your goals to the Lord and watch your progress grow. Heaven is my ultimate goal, and every day is a process of becoming more Christlike until I reach my destination.

Hopefully, you can apply this lesson to whatever endeavor you may be currently undertaking. Here are a few more thoughts on progress. Slow and steady wins the race, just ask the tortoise. Take time to look back and celebrate what you've already accomplished. Speed isn't everything, just keep going!

<u>Reflection</u>

1. What are some current goals you have for yourself? Have you tried breaking the goal down into smaller, more manageable steps? Do you think this will help you to make progress?
2. Do you feel self-compassion is important? Why or why not?
3. Do we try to push through in our own strength? Or, do we allow God to help us in the ups and downs of life?

LESSON #10
DON'T LOSE FOCUS

Therefore let the one who thinks he stands watch out that he does not fall.

— 1 CORINTHIANS 10:12 (NASB)

On every hike there are large climbs. These are both a blessing and a curse. A blessing because you will see beautiful overlooks and feel satisfied by the accomplishment of the climb. You will feel alive as you peer down the mountain, perched precariously on the two foot wide mantel that is the Appalachian Trail. Not all portions seem death defying, but some do.

The curse is pain you experience as your legs carry you upward and onward. Or, if you're like my beautiful wife, you might have a fear of heights that grips you as you wind along the weathered giants of Appalachia. Michelle usually grips my hand as we travel up these sections. She says her hands tingle and she can't catch her breath as she looks over the edge at a three hundred foot fall. Thankfully as long as my feet are on a steady surface I don't carry this same aversion to heights.

I often look down and think to myself, "I can't believe thousands and thousands of people make this traverse every year and nobody falls from here." Sometimes I'm out hiking with a small daypack, which doesn't shift or throw me off balance like my larger hiking pack. I wonder how much harder the section would be if I were doing it with a full pack.

I have lots of time to think while I'm in the mountains. One of my recurring thoughts revolves around how much time, effort and caution goes into the upward climb, but you could lose all progress, and potentially your life, if you lost focus and slipped over the side. You could climb for hours and fall in seconds. Gravity is a funny thing. This, you see, is the comparison to our lives.

We want to make progress, become better, more Christlike. We climb upward, in our everyday life, making progress, becoming better. Yet, if we aren't careful we lose focus and can give all the progress back in these moments. I know this can happen, I've lived it, I've experienced it in life, and in the last fifteen years of ministry I've witnessed this over and over.

In Isaiah 26:3 we read these words, "I will keep him in perfect peace, whose eye is fixed upon Me, because he trusts in Me." I cannot overstate the importance of not losing focus on Christ as we walk through our daily lives. Just as we are in danger on a mountainside when we allow our minds to wander and our focus to drift from the security of the trail, we are in danger in our spiritual lives when we allow our focus to drift from Christ.

Matthew 14 is a great example of this. Peter, in the

middle of strong winds and waves, trusted Jesus and stepped out of the boat. We can criticize Peter, but he had the courage to step out. Peter didn't just step and stand, he walked forward, took steps on water, and he got close to Jesus. How do I know he got close? The Bible says when Peter began to sink, Jesus reached out His hand and caught Peter and raised him out of the water. Think about it; Peter was right in the middle of a miracle. He was close to Jesus, he was the one with faith, but he began to sink because his focus drifted from Jesus. He took notice of the winds and waves around him. No doubt his mind started to analyze the situation, he was a fisherman and knew this was impossible. He had climbed higher in this moment than any other disciple, yet his life was in danger in the blink of an eye. Why? The answer is simple, he lost focus.

The Apostle Paul expresses this thought another way in Philippians 3:14. He says, "I press towards the mark for the prize." Pressing towards the mark is descriptive of a life focused on a goal. There is a goal, a prize to be had, the reason we do what we do- the high calling of Christ. Is life easy? No, we were never promised it would be easy, but if we continue it will be worth it.

It's easy for my mind to slip back to summers in the late 90's. In my opinion the summers of '95-'99 were some of the greatest days one could have been a teenager. Well, the best days until football practice started.

Football is akin to religion in south Alabama where I grew up. We seemed to have had it dialed in at the little private school I attended. We enjoyed winning seasons and State Championships, but there was a price to be paid. This price was paid in sweat and blood during the hot July and August summer days. Our field sat down in a natural bowl with hills surrounding the stadium. A classic high school stadium called "The Snake Pit." I thought our coaches took great pride in coming up with new and creative ways to teach us the intestinal fortitude the game required. One such lesson involved a hill behind the visitor seating.

This hill was fairly straight up, covered in briars, and probably would be outlawed in today's generation. We formed four lines at the bottom of the hill, and when our coach blew the whistle, we crawled up the hill on our hands and feet. The deal was to keep your knees off the ground, just hands and feet. You crawled up the hill, touched the fence, ran back down the hill, and prepared to climb again. Sometimes we elected to do this drill during our early four o'clock in the morning practice, so it wasn't so hot. Remember, I told you it'd get outlawed today.

As we climbed that hill we would slip. We'd get all scratched up. We tried to pull our socks up high to protect our legs, but inevitably the first group of briars would pull the socks down and our legs would get cut up. We climbed and we climbed. We hurt, it wasn't fun, but if you had your mind right, if you stayed focused on the prize, you made it through those tough days of summer. Then, a few months later, we were Champions.

I recently heard Evangelist Tim Enloe speak. Tim talked about the process of a Spirit empowered life, the struggle to become more Christlike, and he compared it to walking up a mountain. He encouraged people to keep climbing the mountain of God. We get discouraged, absolutely, but we can't stop. We must stay focused on the climb, stay focused on Christ, and stay focused on our ultimate goal.

John Stephen Akhwari was a marathon runner from the country of Tanzania. He was one of 75 competitors running in the 1968 Olympic marathon in Mexico City. Some time during the race he experienced altitude sickness due to the change in elevation from his home. Then, he tripped in a crowd and fell, which resulted in him injuring his shoulder and his knee. His knee was bleeding and appeared to be dislocated. Medical staff encouraged him to withdraw. His run turned into a slow limp, and he fell off the pace. He entered the Olympic stadium over an hour after the leaders. Actually, the medal ceremony was concluding and few spectators remained in attendance. When interviewed afterwards he stated, "My country did not send me 10,000 miles just to start the race; they sent me to finish the race."[1] What an illustration. We must keep our focus, climb our mountain, fight the good fight, and finish our race.

<u>Reflection</u>

1. Have you ever found yourself in a precarious situation that required your total focus? How does that relate to your day to day walk with God?
2. What are the consequences in your life from lacking focus on Christ?
3. What are some habits you can adopt to ensure you keep your eyes fixed daily on the Lord?

LESSON #11
HE WATCHES OVER YOU

For he will command his angels concerning you to guard you in all your ways.

— PSALM 91:11 ESV

In the Summer of 2022, we were blessed to have a group of Southeastern University students come to work with us. This was a week-long mission trip. We fed hikers, removed tons (literally tons) of debris from the lot, and ministered at local hostels. As we neared the end of the time, the group wanted to do a section hike and spend one night camping on the Appalachian Trail.

We chose to do the six mile section that runs from Tennessee Highway 91 over to Low Gap. This is the section of trail that is very near us, ending only three miles from the lot in Shady Valley. Our destination for the night would be Double Springs shelter. Aptly named due to the double piped spring that offers a reliable flow of water year round.

We got to the shelter and began setting up camp. The guys elected to stay in the two man tent in front of the shelter. The girls and my son, Lane, decided they wanted to hammock camp directly behind the shelter, and we had one neighbor who was camping further up the hill behind them. I never get to sleep in shelters much, so I made the choice to sleep on the platform of the shelter. This allowed me a good vantage point between my slightly spread out group of young people. As night fell we made a fire, sang songs, did communion, and eventually made our way into our sleeping bags for the night. Except I didn't really go to sleep, because I knew some information they didn't know.

Almost all hikers now have an app on their phone that allows them to understand distance, find water, and has a GPS location. This app also allows you to place notes to be shared with other hikers for each shelter, water source, hostel, and area along the trail. I knew we were camping very close to the Kettlefoot Bear Sanctuary, and took notice of some recent reports on the app that listed bear activity in our general area.

I get questions about bears all the time. Black bears are the only bears in the mountain ranges of the eastern United States. Even when an area or bear is listed as problematic, it is rare to have any real physical attacks. Mostly they are interested in your food or other exotic smells like toothpaste. The bears in Kettlefoot come in two varieties, the local bears and the town bears. The local bears are wild, well muscled, rarely seen, and very skittish around humans. These aren't the ones I worry about.

The town bears are the ones I worry will lumber into my campsite unannounced. These bears likely grew up farther south, near Gatlinburg and Pigeon Forge. These bears are usually bigger than local bears because of the city diet, and they are much less afraid of people. In town they ate from dumpsters, became acclimated to tourists, raided garbage cans, and rode roller coasters at Dollywood until they became such a nuisance the Tennessee Wildlife Resources Agency relocated them. The Cherokee National Forest that surrounds our lot, and Kettlefoot Bear Sanctuary which borders us, is a common destination for releasing the bears back into the wilderness. A place where human interaction is less common, unless you are a hiker with food, bugspray, and fruity smelling lotions. We checked these boxes.

I'm sure everyone went to sleep, or tried to sleep, saying a prayer for protection and safety from bear encounters, but nobody had the information I had. Sure, bears can be anywhere in Appalachia, but I knew they could be close. I did not feel threatened or unsafe, but I didn't want to deal with the drama of a bear encounter, and I wouldn't want to tell Pastor Draughon I'd let a university student get mauled. So I decided for most of the night I'd sit at watch and keep a light close. As I looked back over this night I saw so many parallels to God's watchful eye over His children.

For starters, the Bible is clear in Psalm 121 God doesn't slumber or sleep. I have known people who deal with anxiety and have sleepless nights. I always tell them they can give it to God and go to sleep, because He'll stay awake and handle it. Just as I decided I was going to stay up most of the night to watch over my group, the Lord does the same for you. Give your troubles to the Lord, He's going to be up all night anyway.

Also, people usually worry about what might be in the dark. The unseen danger. Perhaps the team was praying there would be no late night visitors in camp. But they didn't have all the information, I did. I used this information to best guide the experience and make sure everyone was safe. I know there are times when I pray about things, aches and pains, safety on road trips, all sorts of things. Even though I'm aware there could be an issue, I don't have all the information. I can't predict the future. I trust God has all the information, He knows best how to guide me, and He is working all things out for my good.

It is important to remember how often the Bible uses the analogy of the sheep and shepherd. We are told God is the good shepherd. In John 10:11 Jesus states, "I am the good shepherd. The good shepherd sacrifices His life for the sheep."[1] The shepherd's job was to care for the sheep. He would sit and watch day and night. He was ready to confront the bear or lion that would appear. He protected his sheep from pestilence, heat, cold, and drought. He was an expert at knowing if they needed shade in the heat, or a sunny field to warm from the cold. A good shepherd would die for his sheep, just as Christ died for us, to cleanse our sins. When you are uncertain remember he watches over you.

If you go and study scripture you might be able to discern just how much this topic relates to shepherding. Go and study scripture verses on God watching over you, and sleep. What you will find is interesting. Psalms, and the writings of David are littered with these references. Go read Psalms 143, 121, 3 and 4 just to name a few. David was a shepherd, he watched over sheep, and this was the perfect way for him to explain God's watchful eye over his children.

Honestly, I believe God protects us from things we will never know anything about. He's tripped more traps in front of me, and undone more potential snares than I will ever know. He's healed your body and kept you safe.

I also think this is a reason David was a worshiper. He understood walking in the protection of the Lord. He had been protected from the lion, the bear, and the Philistine giant. He knew what God had done, and knew God protected him from enemies he never knew about. You see, worship and worry can't be friends. They don't hang out together. When we worship, we free ourselves from worry. Worship gets our focus off the issues and troubles of life, and puts our focus back on the Lord. I imagine the young shepherd David sitting out in the field. No doubt a young boy in a field at night with wild animals would have been a scary time. Predators all around him. What did he do? He worshiped the Lord, because worship escorts worry right out the door.

I laid there in the shelter that night. I played some worship music in my headphones, and prayed no bears would come near my dwelling or my people. Then, my eyes got heavy and I went to sleep. It wasn't an accidental sleep, but a peaceful sleep, because I knew if God was going to be awake watching over us there was no reason for both of us to be awake.

<u>Reflection</u>

1. Have you ever experienced a situation that left you troubled to the point you couldn't sleep?
2. Reflect on God's watchful eye. I offered several verses from Psalms, read those and find a few more. Do these words help you in feeling anxious?
3. Remember a time you found freedom in worship. How does this prepare you for future warfare against the flesh?

LESSON #12
DON'T LET THE OIL RUN OUT

"In truth, I have done nothing alone. God has called me and has been my pilot. The Holy Spirit has been my comforter, my guide, and my power source."

— REINHARD BONNKE

In late July 2022 the eastern area of Kentucky experienced historic flooding. Historic because the waters crested over a foot above the hundred year floodplain, meaning there was likely not a soul alive that had ever seen the water get that high. There were areas where complete towns were washed away. As a missionary working in southwestern Virginia, I felt it was only right for me to assist these communities in some way.

There is a hibachi chef in Dothan, AL, affectionately called Joe Cook, that has made it one of his missions to cook for communities impacted by disasters. Joe loads all the supplies and travels hundreds of miles to the areas to bless the locals with a wonderful meal. I saw he was heading to eastern Kentucky and messaged him asking if I could help. It was perfect timing, he needed an assistant and I happened to be near the area he was heading. God was bringing two south Alabama boys together to meet needs in a disaster area of Kentucky.

I determined I would take the drinks because the chef was taking the food. I went down to the local dollar store, because who doesn't have a dollar store? Once again Pug was with me. We both loaded several carts with sodas, water and juice drinks for children. Then, Pug got to witness something I see often as a missionary, something he probably thought I was making up. What he saw was God paying the bill. Everywhere I go I tell people, "If it's God's will, it's God's bill."

As we loaded the drinks, I was calculating how much this haul was going to cost. Not because I was completely broke, or lacked faith, but it's smart to know what you're spending. There is always the Phillip and Andrew debate. In John 6 we see Jesus preparing to feed the multitude. Phillip is calculating and says two hundred denarii couldn't feed them all. Basically two hundred days of wages couldn't feed the group. Then Andrew brings a boy over with five barley loaves and two fish. Obviously this was not enough, this was actually a laughable amount of food for the crowd. I can imagine I would have hung my head embarrassed if I'd seen Andrew bring a boy's lunch to Jesus. We can either sit and calculate, or trust the Lord He can take a little and make a lot happen with it. Be more like Andrew and less like Phillip.

Side note for Pastors, and probably everyone else

I have nothing against budgets, it's just part of being a good steward of the money God has blessed your ministry with. However, when everything is done with rigid calculation, and adherence to numbers alone, you are likely missing out on opportunities to see the miraculous happen. Be sure to leave room for obedience to the Holy Spirit's leading in all financial endeavors.

****Thank you for listening to my Talk****

So, as I was calculating how much money I needed to purchase the drinks for the folks over in Kentucky, my phone dinged in my pocket. It was one of my mission supporters telling me they were sending money, a couple hundred dollars. Randomly, out of the blue, on a Saturday night, here's some money they felt led to send. My brother looked at me and said, "Well, I've heard you talk about stuff like this happening, and now I've seen it." The Lord paid the bill.

The next morning I headed for Kentucky. The trail doesn't go through Kentucky, so I'd never ventured into this area before - it was eye opening. Coal mining had sustained the local economy for years. As I drove through the hollers I passed remnants of the past. Closed mines rusting and fenced off. I wondered what type of jobs were left in this area.

As I approached the town of Fleming Neon I could see the destruction. I had to pull into side lanes bypassing road washouts. I saw cars in trees and homes marked with red X's allowing first responders to know they had already been checked for survivors. The little town looked like a bomb had gone off. Debris piled high, there was no more two lane road, just a path you used to wind through town. Thousands of books pulled from the library covered in mud lined one side ahead of storefronts with shattered windows. I'd honestly never seen anything like this.

In east Kentucky the mountain elevation is lower, but the mountains are very rugged. The only flat land for houses is by the creek which had cut lanes through the mountains for hundreds of years. This presented the problem. Water flowed quickly down these jagged mountain sides into the creeks. The houses were just feet away from the creeks and completely surrounded by mountains that funneled the water downhill. The flood came in the middle of the night, which I believe contributed to the loss of life. This area has little cell service, few weather radios, and for some the first evidence of the high water was feeling the house move underneath them.

I arrived at my destination that sunny Sunday morning feeling a mixture of sorrow and awe. Sorrow for the destruction, and awe at the amazing people of eastern Kentucky. They banded together, helped their neighbors, and were just good salt of the earth folks.

It occurs to me I was blessed with a particular upbringing that allows me to move seamlessly among the people of Appalachia and appreciate their traditions. I lived my younger childhood in the small southern town of Elamville, AL. It was a one stoplight town full of characters you could write books about. The old timers told tales of feuds and squabbles that ended in knife fights and violence. Just a few families, and their descendants, made up the majority of the small population. If you weren't from there you had no reason to be there, and folks might let you know it. We sat on the porch with neighbors and watched the sun go down while old dogs milled about in the yard. It was a slower pace of life and a beautiful childhood. Despite its wild and rugged history, Elamville had more churches per capita than most places. When I earned my MBA from Troy University I had them list Elamville as my hometown even though I moved away when I was fourteen. A nod to the old times, and the place that helped build me. I wondered if God had this planned all along. You could have picked Elamville, AL up and sat it down in Knott County, KY or Cocke County, TN, and it would have been a seamless fit. So, when people in Appalachia catch the deep southern drawl and say, "You didn't grow up round here," I usually reply, "No sir, but I grew up close."

We set up outside an old diner that had shut down. We would use this parking lot for cooking and the volunteers, some who themselves had lost everything, would help package the food for their neighbors. We formed an assembly line of sorts. Then it happened. Joe uttered a line I told him was sure to make my next book, he looked at me and said, "In Hibachi oil is very important. Your main job, the most important thing for you to do, is make sure the oil doesn't run out."

I almost busted out in a little dance. Of course he had no clue the cord he'd just struck with his new Bapticostal helper. I grew up Southern Baptist and now I'm an Assembly of God missionary. I jokingly tell people I'm Bapticostal, and that is a Baptist chassis with a Pentecostal motor dropped in it. Regardless, his statement did light a fire in me. I pondered the words for the better part of the day.

In 1 Samuel 16:13 the prophet states, "Then Samuel

took the horn of oil and anointed him in the midst of his brothers; and the Spirit of the Lord came upon David from that day forward. So Samuel arose and went to Ramah." (NKJV) The Holy anointing oil was used as part of the ordination into the priesthood, on the instruments of the tabernacle, and eventually included as part of selecting the next king. As we see in the verse from 1st Samuel the oil was poured and the Holy Spirit came upon David, hence the connection is made with oil symbolizing the work of the Holy Spirit.

In this way power for ministry work is associated with anointing from the Spirit of God. Isaiah 61:1 proclaims, "The Spirit of the Lord is upon me, because the Lord has anointed me to proclaim good news to the poor. He has sent me to bind up the brokenhearted, to proclaim freedom for the captives and release from darkness for the prisoners." (NIV) This was not a literal anointing with oil but an internal anointing that sprang from the encounter Isaiah had in Isaiah 6. In Acts, Jesus tells his followers to wait until they are endued with power and then they will be his witnesses locally, regionally, and into all the world. However, don't start until you have received what you need from God, endued with Holy Spirit power.

You see the Holy Spirit is the spark in our Christian walk. I know I'm probably about to make somebody mad, but if you've gotten this far you can handle it. I have nothing against education, I love education, I want to go back and get more education, but we can't rely on education to give us the spark to do the work of the Lord. I've heard it said and know it's true, eight cylinders in a truck are no better than two if you don't have a spark in the engine. If you mix that spark of the Spirit with the education, now you've got something! A degree may get you a job, but only the empowering work of the Holy Spirit gives you the boldness to slay the giant. Saul had the job, David had the anointing.

While we're here, let's go a little further. Why did they anoint kings? Kings would be the decision makers for the people, and it was important for kings to have clarity and unction from the Spirit in order to make the correct decisions leading the people. You want to know why some churches get in a mess? Why do they make business decisions instead of walking by faith? They allow individuals who don't have the anointing of the Spirit to serve on deacon boards and in positions of leadership. These individuals are the decision making body for the community of believers and don't have the mind of Christ. Carnal people will never be able to make spiritual decisions.

Another reason you can't let the oil run out in your spiritual life involves knowledge and truth. 1 John 2:27 tells us, "But the anointing that you received from Him abides in you, and you have no need that anyone should teach you. But as His anointing teaches you about everything, and is true, and is no lie, just as it has taught you, abide in Him." (ESV) The Holy Spirit teaches you. Believing the writers of the Bible did so as inspired by the Holy Spirit, I often use the following illustration. If you were taking a literature class and studying Huckleberry Finn, would you gain more from listening to your teacher lecture on the book, or from sitting and hearing from Mark Twain himself? Without a doubt, if you sit with the writer you would learn things about the work a professor could never teach you. In the same way, when we read Scripture we are able to communicate directly with the writer, the Holy Spirit. He teaches us and leads us into all understanding.

Today, we know that the anointing of the Spirit is available to all. Any Christian will tell you they know when they are feeling depleted. Perhaps they don't pray as they should, or fell out of the habit of reading the Bible. Listen to me believer, your most important job is to make sure the oil doesn't run out. My truck runs good, but if I never serviced the oil, I guarantee in about ten thousand miles I'll be sitting on the side of the road because the oil got old and stale. Don't let your oil get old and stale, and don't let it run out.

<u>Reflection</u>

1. Can you remember a time when God touched your life, filled you with his Holy Spirit, and empowered you for Christian living?
2. What activities create extra stress and cause our oil to become old and stale? Why is it important to get a periodic "oil service"?
3. Can you look back on your life and see the hand of God in your formative years, leading you into your current roles?
4. In what way has the Holy Spirit led you into a deeper understanding of Scripture? Note: the Spirit will never lead you in a direction contrary to God's word.

LESSON #13
GOD'S PROTECTION

"Through many dangers, toils and snares, I have already come; 'Tis grace has brought me safe thus far and grace will lead me home."

— JOHN NEWTON

If you read my first book then you might be wondering why I would include another lesson on God's protection. Perhaps it's because, if you're like me, I didn't get the message clear the first time. Or, maybe it's because I have another amazing story to tell. One thing is clear, every missionary has many of these stories. I've been amazed to hear them, and thankful to live through a few.

Recently, I was driving back to Alabama on a return trip from our mountain property. I always try to avoid getting gas in the cities, or anywhere near a city. I will pay a few cents extra to avoid Knoxville, Chattanooga, and Atlanta urban areas when pumping gas. That seems paranoid, but you will see my reasoning soon enough. There are issues that come with these city gas stations.

As I drove I was thinking about the 100 mile hike we had just completed. I was contemplating the intineration season we were in, and doing some praying in the truck. All these things seemed to distract me from my fuel gauge which did not catch my eye until it dinged. This ding lets me know I'm fifty miles until empty, but I know it drops precipitously once it hits fifty, so I needed to find a station soon. I was just outside Knoxville, but still too close for my comfort when I found a travel center. I stepped out and paid at the pump like I always do. It's also my habit to leave my driver's side door open a little and stand with my back to my truck. This allows me to see everything in front of me and nothing sneaks up behind me.

Suddenly, as I stood pumping gas, a man kind of jumped out from behind the pump. I didn't see him walk over, so I assume he was hidden behind it and just came around. He was dirty and in disarray. He had sores on his face and arms which are usually tell-tale signs of drug use in this area. I quickly prayed to myself not wanting to miss a divine appointment if the Lord had set this up, but I didn't get a great feeling.

The fellow immediately asked me for money. I have nothing against giving people money to help. Sometimes I'll buy food, sometimes I might give a small sum of money. What they do with the money is on them, I just try to be obedient to the Holy Spirit, but once again, I wasn't feeling it here. I replied I was heading south on the last leg of my trip, and didn't have cash money on me. This wasn't a lie, but he persisted.

"Come on man, my girl ran off and left me in a bad

spot. Before she left she drove all the gas out of our car and I'm trying to go to work. Help me out man."

Again, I told him I didn't have any money on me and couldn't help this time. I noticed him sway and reach into his pocket. Unknown to him I reached my hand down to the one weapon I actually carry with me. A knife I keep in my driver's side door.

This isn't just any knife. A friend I'd met through another friend had given me this knife from his collection when I first went on the mission field. It's a big, nice knife, weighted perfectly for outdoor use. A type of trapper's knife. I instinctively put my hand on this knife when the fellow went to his pocket and pulled out a closed knife of his own.

"Hey man, I got this knife. Let me sell you this knife. Here hold this pocket knife and see how good it feels."

"I don't need a knife."

"Come on man, buy this knife."

"I'm not buying your knife, I don't need a knife."

Then, before I knew what was happening, he opened the knife and held it forward in a threatening manner.

"What if someone pulled a knife on you? I bet you'd need a knife then," he said.

Thankfully, I already had my hand on my knife. My big, impressive, sharp, outdoor knife. I pulled my right hand out of my truck to reveal it.

I held my knife up in front of my chest and said, "I think if someone pulled a knife on me, I could handle it."

My new friend immediately jumped back. "Woah, woah, you're right, you're right. That's a knife right there. You don't need this knife, nope. I'm not even gonna sell you this knife.

With that he darted around the gas pumps and across the parking lot. I stopped the pump and drove away. I didn't see where he went, but I didn't want to give him any second chance ideas. It happened so smoothly and fast. Once I was in my truck driving away I got a little shaky. I called Michelle and told her I'd just had to pull my knife on a guy at the gas pump. Wow! I've never before had anything like that happen to me.

One of the questions I get the most is if I carry a gun with me while I'm in the field. The answer is always the same, no. There are so many laws regarding guns that change from state to state and wilderness area to national park. Usually when the family travels our dogs go with us. These aren't ankle biters; we have two Doberman Pinschers named Bella and Baxter. No matter the situation, we choose to place our safety and security in the hands of the Lord.

There is a phrase I often share with people. I have said this for as long as I can remember, but I can't remember where I first heard it. Forgive me if I tread here without a proper citation, but this is a mantra I live by. "For the servant of God, safety is not geographical, it's theological." Basically this means the will of God is the safest place you can find yourself. What if God called you to a dangerous foreign land, or an unsafe inner city to serve? Is that safer than choosing to live your life in disobedience to God? Any missionary will tell you it is far safer to live in the will of God than with the safety and ease of a comfortable place.

Psalms 91 is one of my favorite passages of Scripture. The whole chapter resounds with the hope of God's protection. It begins, "He who dwells in the secret place of the Most High, shall abide under the shadow of the Almighty. I will say of the Lord, "He is my refuge and fortress; My God, in Him will I trust." (Psalm 91:1-2 NKJV)

We can learn much about safety from Psalm 91.

Where you position your life is important. The Psalmist is clear, our proximity to the Lord equates to safety. If you stand in someone's shadow then you need to be fairly close to the individual. Which sheep do you think is safest when the wolf comes? The one who is near the shepherd, or the one that has wandered far from the flock? Does closeness to God equal no stress, no attacks, a problem free life? Of course not. I tried to be close to the Lord and still had a guy pull a knife on me. However, I know that the Lord was with me, and I was not afraid.

Look at the imagery of the Psalmist. God is his refuge and fortress. A fortress is an impenetrable wall surrounding you. A place you can run to. In old times workers would go out to the field outside the walls of the castle to tend crops. If trouble were coming a bell would sound and the people would run back into the fortress. The Lord is the place we run to. He's open and ready to shield us from the enemy.

I can't talk about Psalm 91 without mentioning one of my favorite stories. I've heard this told, but once again I can't remember who told it. The imagery is powerful and it stays with me.

There was a wildfire out west. The fire swept through the forests and canyons destroying everything in its path. The next day firefighters walked through this burned out area knocking down any remaining hotspots of fire. Many trees still stood smoldering. As they walked something unusual happened, they saw movement from the base of a tree. Amazingly, small birds began to appear from inside the hollow of a tree stump. These little birds had their lives saved by their mother, who gathered them behind her wings, stood in front of the hollow opening, shielded them from the fire, and lost her life in the process.

Wow! Think about that for a second. We live free because Christ died for us with His arms stretched wide on the cross. We have the promise of protection, hiding under the shadow of His outstretched arms. Do I worry about bears, snakes, or knife wielding assailants? No, and I never will. I have peace. The Lord is watching over me and hiding me under His wings, and He will do the same for you.

<u>Reflection</u>

1. I told you about my gas station encounter. Can you think of a time when the Lord was there for you, protecting you in a dangerous situation? I encourage you to share this testimony with others.
2. What are your thoughts on the quote, "Safety is theological not geographical?"
3. Are you close to the Shepherd? Or do you find yourself walking around the edges of the flock? What changes can you make to get closer to the good Shepherd?

LESSON #14
READING THE RINGS

"Between every two pines is a doorway to a new world."

— JOHN MUIR

What do you know about Dendrochronology? If you're like me you have no clue what that word even means. I knew nothing about it until I started researching for the story I'm about to tell. Dendrochronology is the study of tree rings, and if you know how to read these rings they tell amazing stories.

Wood piles are common sights in the mountains and anywhere in the northeast. I know a few folks in Alabama who have large wood piles, but nothing like these massive stacks I find when traveling further north. The supply of wood you have on hand could make or break your heating in the winter. In some places your survival depends on cutting and stacking wood all summer to prepare for winter. I've seen people stack wood under porches, in funny criss cross patterns, under tarps, and in old barns.

I've never been that interested in wood, but being around so much stacked wood allowed me some time to investigate things. I always look at the rings and try to estimate how old the tree was. That was the extent of what I knew about tree rings. Little did I know there is a world of information to be gained by looking at the annual growth rings of trees.

My first observation really hit close to home. I saw a log that had a very interesting pattern in the rings. It began with nice, tight growth rings that started in the center and moved outward. Somewhere about halfway through the life of the tree were two or three rings that were black and rotted looking. Then it went right back to good growth for the next twenty or so rings to finish its life. I wondered aloud why the tree had two perfect circles of rot surrounded by good growth before and after.

"That's cause the tree had a couple bad years," was the response that came from the property caretaker.

"Like what?" I asked.

"Coulda been anything; a fire, a parasite, something might have happened with the weather."

Now I had something to think about. I thought about my own life. If someone could cut me down and look at the rings of my life, what would they see? They would see exactly the same thing I saw in that tree. Some really good years to start, then some rotten years, followed by more really good years.

I shared my testimony earlier but I'll pull back the curtain again. It can be a little shocking to some that I wasn't always a minister of the gospel. I've shared my story in church, and people have asked if I forgot my children were in the audience. I always tell them I hide nothing from my kids and hope they gain wisdom from my short-comings and not go down the same road. I had a rough year or two. I want you to get this lesson, the lesson from this tree and my life. A couple bad years does not disqualify you from a promising life.

The enemy tries to tell anyone who makes a mistake they are done. They can't be redeemed. There is no hope left for happiness and usefulness in the service of the Lord. We meet lots of people who are wandering around in this state. Truth be told, we are too quick to write off people in this state. A couple bad years does not spell the end; hold your head up!

Another interesting observation is when the rings are very close on one side and very wide on the other side. The center circle is moved far to one side from the center. It's said when you see this the tree was likely leaning over for a long period of time and grew crooked. This off center growth is literally called the tree "not having its heart in the right place." Its center was out of line.

You see where I'm going with this. The trees whose hearts aren't in the right place are the leaning trees and will eventually become blowdowns. This relates to our life perfectly. The only reason I'm where I am today is because I gave my heart to Jesus. Not my physical heart of course, but the center of my being. My soul is the Lord's. When the center of our life is misaligned we open ourselves up to destruction. When the wind of life blows in just the right direction we have no defense. [1]

The Bible is clear about the heart. Ezekiel 36:26 says " And I will give you a new heart, and a new spirit I will put within you. And I will remove the heart of stone from your flesh and give you a heart of flesh." (ESV) The prophet Jeremiah states the heart is deceitful and sick. In a spiritual sense we are all born with a heart condition. We are all born leaning and likely to become a blowdown. In this condition God alone can change the hard heart of man.

It's an often said and overused illustration, but allow me to use it again. Some people have a "head" knowledge of God but not a "heart" knowledge of God. They know scripture, they can quote sections of the Bible, grew up in church and have taken communion. They have gone through the motions and look the part, but they really don't have a true heart relationship with the Savior.

In his sermon "Divine and Supernatural Light," Jonathan Edwards uses the following illustration. He says, "Your mind can know honey is sweet, people can tell you it's sweet, you've read books about it, etc., but if you haven't actually tasted it, you know with your head, but not with your heart."[2] Have you ever tasted something and had to sit back and enjoy the goodness of it? A strawberry so sweet it catches you by surprise. A steak perfectly cooked. There is a difference in hearing about it, and tasting it for yourself.

Please note, when I say heart knowledge, I'm not talking about emotion. I get emotional talking about the Lord, there's nothing wrong with that. Nobody cares when you are emotional on Saturday over a football game, but people lose their minds if they see a little emotion on Sunday. Emotion isn't bad, but emotion doesn't save you. Only a clear heart knowledge of Christ as Savior and Lord does that. Now you can get a little emotional about that.

So, I guess I'm an amateur Dendrochronologist. Truth be told, I see God in everything, even tree growth rings.

Remember, a few bad years does not equal the end for you. I hope you don't have those, I'd love for every young person who reads this to have steady growth with no rot. If you find yourself in a place of trouble, having a few bad or hard years, just know it doesn't have to be the end. Spend time with Jesus, get your heart right, let Him straighten and strengthen the tree, and grow to your full potential.

<u>Reflection</u>

1. In what ways do you see God in your everyday life?
2. What do these observations tell you about the character of God?
3. Spend some time looking up different trees mentioned in the Bible. What jumps out at you about the trees?

LESSON #15

SEEING THE POSSIBILITY

"Most people are not really free. They are confined by the niche in the world that they carve out for themselves. They limit themselves to fewer possibilities by the narrowness of their vision."

— V.S. NAIPAUL

The backstory of our lot in Shady Valley is a tale all of its own. Michelle and I had envisioned what we would like to do for hikers while driving home from our first visit to Trail Days in 2019. We'd love to have a place where they could shower, get some food, and stay with us for a night or two. A waypoint in the middle of the long thru hike. A free blessing to share the love of Jesus and bless them on the journey. The dream hit a hard reality very quickly.

The real estate market in the mountains near the Appalachian Trail is hot. I don't mean let it cool before you put it in your mouth hot, I'm talking liquid lava hot. I recently saw a 650 square foot, sixty five year old house that needed some work, on a quarter acre in Damascus, VA going for $160,000. This was 1 bedroom, 1 bath. This is not the market for our missions budget with needs for a house to hold kids and live. So we decided that a vacant lot of land somewhere in the area might be a better deal.

Our search had a depressing beginning. Due to not being able to afford anything near town we had to head into the surrounding countryside. The countryside where there is no internet, no cell phone service, and not very close to hikers. This posed multiple problems. Our poor realtor tried her best to secure an acre or two within our budget, but we didn't give her much to work with. She showed us some land on a mountainside; we'd need an excavator to level off a small spot for a cabin, and the driveway would have been straight up. It was not looking good. I gave her my wishlist. I'd love something you could pull straight into, no large mountain going up the driveway. Cell service and internet were a necessity with us home-schooling kids and trying to stay connected to hikers and the world. An existing septic tank would be nice, because putting a septic tank into the rocky soil of Appalachia costs twice as much as it does in south Alabama. Lastly, if it were a desire of my heart kind of thing, I'd love some type of stream or water feature. Ask anyone who has looked for land in the Appalachian mountains about my wishlist and limited budget. I'm sure their reply would be something along the lines of "good luck." But you don't need luck when you've got the Lord.

I was hanging out with Boxcar one day when I received a phone call. It was a fellow who wanted to show me some land in Shady Valley, TN. This was beautiful land with two barns. The property was several acres, but the price tag was vastly more than my limited budget could handle. I told him we just couldn't swing it. The location was perfect, just a few miles into Tennessee from Damascus, VA. Only three miles or so from the Appalachian Trail. I was torn. Then the fellow says, "I've got the place you've been looking for, but I don't know if I can let it go." It was just up the road. I asked him to show it to me.

We drove into the lot, a straight shot off the road. I could hear the water from the creek that runs along the back of the overgrown property. There was standing water in the front of the drive, knee high weeds, and the remnants of a house that had burned down on the property, old nails and broken glass. But it had it all. Perfect cell service, a stream, a flat open lot, high speed internet from Boone, NC was available, and a brand new septic tank. It was overgrown, needed some work, you had to watch your step for all the rocks and glass, but this was the spot. It checked all the boxes.

We struck a deal that day, a fair deal. I knew there was going to be a good amount of work involved in rehabbing this property, but often your God given dreams and destiny come packaged in hard work. It's part of the deal. I stood in the middle of the lot, in a pile of broken glass, river rock, and weeds past my knee thinking of the possibilities. It occurred to me this was something new God was teaching me. I have not always been able to see what could be. Here are a few things that have helped me see the possibilities.

I've been blessed to hang out with people who see the possible. This is one of the most important aspects for someone like myself. Having friends who are craftsmen, who have vision and skills to make the vision a reality. I looked around our little acre and knew we could turn it into something special, because I'd been around people who made something from nothing. No matter your age, the people you allow to influence you will make or break you. If you spend time with creative dreamers, you tend to dream a little bigger. If you spend time with negative naysayers, you tend to become negative about the prospects in front of you. If you know people who see the possibility in every impossibility, the dreamers, then learn everything you can from them.

Here's another lesson, I've learned details matter. I've always been more of a big picture guy. Finding the lot, making the deal, dreaming about bunkhouses and cabins, big stuff. That's always been my thing. How are you going to make those things happen? That's the details. We had to develop a plan of action. There were so many rocks you couldn't cut the lot with a mower or a bush hog. We began to weed eat in sections, moving rocks as we went from one section to the next. When we got the grass low enough we ran a big magnet over the ground to get the nails and screws up. If you've never cut waist high grass and weeds with a weed eater for about an acre, you should try it. It'll make you appreciate your lawn mower.

If you want to be the person that sees possibility, you have to be prepared for unexpected obstacles. As I cut the grass back I realized there were mounds of dirt pushed over to the side of the lot. I'm going to get into this in the next chapter, but I wasn't expecting to unearth large piles of dirt filled with trash. Then we began to find shingles, and more glass, and carpet. I learned areas of Appalachia don't have garbage pickup and many people don't want to drive over the mountain to the closest dump, so vacant properties in the area become quasi dumps. People at some point had just dumped loads of shingles, old broken blocks, and household junk onto the property. You have to expect obstacles, and not be discouraged when they come your way.

There is another way to look at possibilities. That's to be able to see the possibility in people. Our lot wasn't much to look at that first day. It wasn't much to look at for several months. It took almost a year to get the standing water situation rectified. We still occasionally find glass near the creek, or a piece of household junk works its way to the surface. Those things aside, it's a very nice place now.

I think about my life. There was a time when I was a lot like that piece of ground. I didn't have much possibility in the eyes of some. Sometimes I'll see an old friend doing well, serving the Lord, and I'll act surprised. I'll say something like, "Wow, I'd have never thought he'd serve the Lord and be doing so well in life." Then Michelle looks at me and smiles that sweet smile and says, "You know, people say the same thing about you." One of the great challenges in life, and ministry, is to see the possibility in every person. If I asked everyone today who knew me growing up where they saw me in twenty years, most people say they aren't surprised. These sweet people have forgotten most of what they knew about me. People tend to make you what they want you to be in their memories. If you could have asked them twenty years ago if I'd travel the country preaching, selling devotional books about my ministry to hikers, serving and blessing travelers wherever I go, I don't think they'd ever have been able to envision it.

I couldn't have envisioned it. Thankfully, there were some, even back then, who believed in me and saw the possibility when I couldn't see it myself. Parents of friends, coaches, teachers, people from my church, professors, pastors and evangelists, and company executives who pushed me. They held my feet to the fire, made me believe. They were encouragers who saw the possibility.

A great Biblical example of seeing possibility is Barnabas in Acts. Barnabas' name means son of encouragement. He was an encouragement to others. We learn from the text Paul and Barnabas went out on a missionary trip taking Mark with them. Scholars are mixed on the reasoning, but at a point in the missionary journey Mark left and went home. Later, Barnabas wanted to take Mark on another trip, give him another chance, but Paul refused to take the youngster. Opting instead to take Silas, and Barnabas took Mark. Barnabas saw the possibility in Mark and was willing to make an investment into his life.

In time, Paul and Mark reconciled. Mark is included in Paul's list of greetings in Philemon, describing him as a fellow laborer. Later, Paul writes in 2 Timothy 4:11 that Mark was profitable to him in ministry. If not for Barnabas seeing the possibility in Mark, would we have the Gospel of Mark? I want to encourage you to see the possibility. See the potential in places, in dreams, and in people. You never know what that bad little kid in your church, the addict, or the down on their luck, mistake riddled Christian will become if you encourage them and give them a chance. See the possibilities in people.

I am forever thankful for the pastors, teachers, and friends who saw possibility in me. I wasn't voted "Most Likely to Succeed," and most at one time or another might have questioned what positive impact I'd make on the world. The likelihood of Brad Sasser traveling the world speaking for Jesus, hiking mountains sharing the Gospel, serving food to strangers, and positively impacting lives was never zero. However, the odds weren't good. I appreciate the ones who challenged me to be better, didn't let me make excuses, and helped me reach my potential. I strive daily to do that for others.

<u>Reflection</u>

1. We encountered several roadblocks in our original search. Think of a time when you hit roadblocks that were actually God redirecting you to His intended answer.
2. Why is having vision for the possible important for a believer's own life?
3. Why is having vision for the potential of others also important?
4. How is your mindset affected when you encounter unexpected surprises in your work/dreams?

LESSON #16
STOP HIDING YOUR TRASH

"Clutter is not just the stuff on the floor—it's anything that stands between you and the life you want to be living."

— PETER WALSH

I mentioned earlier the trash piles we uncovered at the lot in Shady Valley, but that was only the tip of the iceberg. As I began to dig into the mounds of dirt we started to find old plastic bowls, bottles, broken window panes, and other household debris. At the edges of the stream I was shocked at the amount of broken glass. I knew the previous house on the lot burned down, but I was beginning to think a bomb had exploded. Apparently, the cleanup process included getting it to a certain point and just burying the rest of the debris. It looks pretty good, but underneath is danger and nastiness.

The problem with beginning to uncover debris is you never know how far down the rabbit hole you will go. I have been digging trash out of the ground praying I don't disturb an old grave or find a body. We found old cans of nails, half an old Ford truck, and enough buried carpet to recover a two thousand square foot house. To be fair, the carpet wasn't originally buried, but over the course of time grass had grown over and reclaimed it. In addition to the rubble of the old house, some people use abandoned lots in Appalachia as their own garbage dumps, including this one, so I was dealing with some of this as well.

One day I ventured down to the local country store. Let me tell you about the Shady Valley country store. This is the happening place in Shady Valley, TN. It sits right in the main intersection and is a hub of activity. If you want to know anything you can go down and ask them. If you need to speak with someone in the valley, they have the phone number - or you can sit there long enough and the person will stop by. The country store is part gas station, part souvenir shop, part roadside grill. This is truly the type of place that has died out in most places and been replaced by big chain stores. Not in Shady Valley. It's a local establishment, a true piece of Americana. Imagine your granddaddy's old gas station and the Cracker Barrel had a baby, that's the Shady Valley country store. Anyway, sorry to digress.

I happened into the country store and overheard a couple of the old timers talking. One fellow said, "Yelp, I'm waiting for my son to come over with his tractor, he's gonna help me bury some trash." I couldn't believe what I was hearing, it wasn't just at my place. It's common practice in the area to just bury the old chicken coop, or burn the trash and bury other things you can't burn. I thought, "We've got to stop burying trash because eventually it's going to come back up to the surface and have to be dealt with." That's what we were doing right now; eventually it has to be dealt with. You can't just bury it and hope it never comes up. You must deal with it, haul it off to the dump and be done with it.

I can't help but see the spiritual parallels. In Exodus 2:11-12 we see Moses observe an Egyptian beating a Hebrew slave, one of his own people. This enraged Moses, so he killed the Egyptian taskmaster and buried him in the sand. It wasn't long before his sin was found out. I know some argue if Moses committed a sin here as he was the eventual deliverer of his people, but I believe he did. In this instance he took matters into his own hands and used his fleshly ability to kill the Egyptian. The people would be delivered by God's hand, not the hand of Moses. He sinned and tried to hide it, but it found him out.

I have another old football story I always think about when reminding people that the all seeing eye of the Lord is always upon us. Nothing is done in secret. When we played ball there was a cameraman who would video the game from the pressbox. Now we can video on our phone, but back then it was the old school large video camera on a tripod with a video cassette tape in it. Our coach called this old camera "the one eyed bandit in the sky." We'd watch film of our previous week's game each Monday after school, and we could easily see who was holding or doing anything illegal. Our coach would say, "Boys, the one eyed bandit in the sky don't lie." You were without excuse when the tape played on Monday afternoon; if you messed up in the game they had you. We'd sink low into our chairs when it was pointed out we pulled the wrong way or missed a block. I promise you, the all seeing eye in the sky don't lie. You can't hide it from God, He's got us.

I'm not huge on illustrated sermons when I preach. I've never brought a kitchen table onto the stage, or had six youth stand in a line and do jumping jacks. No problem if you do, I've always wished I were more creative. I'm the guy that refuses to use the new headsets; just give me the handheld microphone and turn me loose. I'm very outside the box, yet old school preacher all wrapped up into one. I myself don't know how it works, but I have this one illustration.

To be honest it wasn't even an illustration of my creation. I stole it from the Evangelist David Ring, and he probably lifted it off someone before. He's just the person I remember from my childhood using it, and it made an impression on me. I don't remember his sermon, but the illustration stayed with me. I haven't done it in ten years, but I still have people come up to me and mention the illustration. People gave their hearts to Jesus that day, that's most important.

For the illustration I went to the Goodwill and got an old dress shirt for two dollars. I went home and took a knife and shredded the back of the shirt. I rubbed dirt on it, and wrote the words shame, liar, fornicator, adulterer, hate, etc. The back of the shirt looked horrible. My wife came in and wondered aloud if I was ok, so I told her about what I'd planned.

For the illustration to work I had to wear a full suit, with coat and tie. I had the shirt on but it was perfect in the front, the part you could see. I preached the whole sermon about the hidden sins from the story of Moses. Is it possible people can have things hidden you had no clue about? Do we do it ourselves every day? What really lies underneath? Near the end of the sermon I took off my coat, careful not to expose my back to the congregation. I stood in front of the altar talking to the church, then I turned around. I exposed the back of the shirt, the dirtiness, the sins, and the tears. Oh the things we hide from everyone.

Just like we eventually had to deal with the trash hidden at the lot, if you're going to walk in freedom you have to deal with the hidden things in your life. I knew I couldn't build anything on top of rubbish; I had to remove the debris before the new building projects started. The same is true in your life. God wants to build anew in you, but you need to allow Him to remove the trash so the new projects can come alive in you. Often I pray God will reveal to me anything that is buried, maybe I've forgotten something I needed to pray about. Things I need to repent and turn from. I've had to go back and ask forgiveness for things I didn't even know were wrong at the time they were done. We've all had to forgive people who don't deserve forgiveness, or maybe we're still needing to forgive.

Sometimes we think we've got most of the trash up then another project uncovers something new. Often your development in Christ will lead you to uncover things progressively. As these new things spring to life we should handle them quickly. Repent, get it behind you, ask for forgiveness, get freedom. If you persist in hiding things it will eventually find you out in this life or eternity. It will cause you trouble in the future, it will cause constant worry, and give the enemy an open door of accusation against you. Close those doors today and get it behind you. God wants to build something new in you.

<u>Reflection</u>

1. Is there anything you have "hidden in the sand" you need to give to the Lord today?
2. Do you have any meaningful sermon illustrations that have stood out to you over the years?
3. Some people are afraid to deal with old wounds because they are afraid of what else might be dug up. Are you affected by this fear? God can help you deal with every hidden and uncovered thing today.

LESSON #17
GOD MAKES A WAY

"God knows better than we do. He always does. Even when it doesn't make sense."

— KAREN KINGSBURY

Once the lot was free from the majority of the debris we were free to work on the projects. One of the main projects we wanted to get done was a bunkhouse. The bunkhouse would be used to house hikers who we built relationships with as they traveled the trail. This building would house ten to twelve hikers at a time. I was hoping to have at least a 16 x 16 foot building to handle this job. There was one big catch.

This was right in the middle of the big price increase in building materials of 2022. There was no shortage of people trying to remind me building materials were going sky high. I'd tell folks I felt now was the time to build the bunkhouse, and immediately they'd tell me about the prices of lumber. I started letting everyone know the same

God who hung the stars in the sky could handle the prices of lumber in 2022. I trusted the Lord and I knew that He was going to come through.

One morning in late summer we awoke and decided we would travel over to Boone, NC for an enjoyable day off trail. On the way back I needed to make a phone call, and was looking for an area with service. My phone dinged, so I pulled over into a gravel drive to make the call. While talking I realized I'd pulled over at a small antique shop. Michelle had been sleeping but she stirred awake. I was in trouble now, she was going to insist we go inside the building.

I begrudgingly agreed since we were taking a day off trail I'd go inside the store. When we entered I was immediately drawn to a couple old barn doors in the back. While admiring the doors the older gentleman who ran the business asked if I liked old wood. Of course I did. It was probably the only thing I was interested in there. He told me there was more wood outside he needed to get rid of.

I couldn't believe what I was looking at when I got outside. He had torn down an old blacksmith shop. Some of the hundred plus year old wood had char marks from the kiln. There were eight foot beams, wide enough for a mantle, hand chopped, with wood pegs still in them.

"Wow, I love this wood you have here, but I doubt I can afford it. How much would you have to have for all of this wood?"

"I'd let it all go today for $100.00."

I couldn't believe my ears. One hundred dollars for all this old wood. A quick google search revealed similar beams on ebay for $500. I bought the wood but couldn't get it all in one load. We decided I'd come back the next day for the rest.

When I got back, the older gentleman helped me load the rest of that old wood. Then he asked what I might be doing with it all. I told him, "I'm going to use it in my bunkhouse." He said, "Oh, you have a bunkhouse." I laughed and told him, "No sir, not yet. I'm going to have one soon, I just need to figure out how to build it." He leaned on the back of my truck and thought for a few seconds. Then he asked, "Would you be willing to work with a 16 X 20 building?" That sounded great to me, so I proceeded, "But what about the cost?" He replied, "Oh, about $800.00."

I couldn't believe what I just heard and agreed to as I drove back to Shady Valley. Everyone said it was going to cost thousands and thousands of dollars. Look at God! Long story short, my brother and I helped him tear it down, so we got it even cheaper. We took it back to the lot, and a group from South Decatur Church of God in Alabama came to help us put it up. We had it up on the lot less than 24 hours after we tore it down. A chance encounter on our day off proved to be the miraculous provision of God.

As I've traveled Alabama as an itinerating missionary I've had a chance to tell that story. I always ask people in the congregations what prayer they're believing the Lord to answer. If He will make an ax head float, and allow me to build a bunkhouse for cheap in the most expensive building material year for a decade, He will come through for you when you need Him.

There are so many examples of God's miraculous provision, of His healing touch, and meeting needs in

Scripture I can barely pick just one. However, I decided to go with a little used miracle, a simple miracle. The story of Jesus paying the tax money owed with a fish, found in Matthew 17:24-27.

A few things to note about the amazing provision in this story. One, this is the only miracle of Christ that resulted in direct monetary gain. Jesus was not in it for the money. He had people who helped Him, they slept on the ground, I'm sure His robes were last year's robes and were out of style. If Jesus were here today He'd probably get his clothes from the Goodwill and Discount Dillards. What Jesus was doing here was meeting a physical monetary need for the disciples they may have been unable to meet for themselves. Remember, these guys are a few years out of work at this time and unemployment pay was a few thousand years away from becoming available.

In this miraculous provision we see Jesus pay a debt for the disciples they owed, but could not pay. Likewise when Christ was crucified on Calvary's cross we see Christ pay a debt for us all we owed, but could not pay. He paid a spiritual debt, and occasionally a physical debt for me as well.

In this story the fish has a degree of compulsion. We know animals obey God. Look at the ravens who fed the prophet Elijah, or the Lions in the lion's den that had their mouths shut for Daniel the whole night. Or the great fish from Jonah who volunteered his services to help a wayward prophet get back on the proper path. It seems there was only two entities in the Bible that had free will to disobey God, men and angels.

I've said it many times, I'm not a prosperity guy. Not everyone is going to drive a new Cadillac and live in a large house. If this was a guarantee to Christians then one, everybody would sign up, and two, God would have to apologize to the Apostles who were thrown into prison, beaten, often paid little, and eventually martyred for the Kingdom's cause. But I love the words of Psalm 37:25, "I have been young, and now am old; yet I have not seen the righteous forsaken, Nor His descendants begging bread." He will take care of you. I'm reminded of such a time in our early marriage.

Michelle was about seven months pregnant with Lane, and I'd just had an MRI on my back. At this time our disposable income was around five dollars per month. We had no savings, and made little money; we were the epitome of "livin' on love." My MRI had a hefty copay, somewhere in the three hundred dollar range. Somehow we paid that, then the washing machine went out. Anyone who's had a baby knows the importance of an operational washing machine when the baby arrives. I can still remember those prayers.

"Lord, what are we going to do?"

"Father, I don't know much about washing machines, but I do know You, and I need some help."

We were starting to come up with contingency plans. Perhaps we'd drive the laundry to our parents house. Maybe go to the laundromat in Clio until we can figure this issue out. None of these scenarios were comforting to a seven month pregnant wife. Then it happened, the miraculous provision of God.

I still remember walking to the mailbox at the old house in Elamville. I saw a letter from the hospital and immediately had a sense of dread come over me. I didn't want to open another letter from the hospital. We were already out of money and could have used that three hundred dollars from the MRI to get a new washer. The last thing I wanted to see was another hospital bill, but it wasn't a bill, it was a check. The letter said we'd already met our deductible, and the hospital was refunding the money collected. I couldn't believe it. Mainly because there was no way we had met our deductible. I showed Michelle the check, and she said it couldn't have been right, but who were we to argue with God. I decided we should cash the check, use the money, and if they rebilled us we would worry about that at a later date. We bought a new washing machine and never heard back from the hospital. Look at God! He's a waymaker and a miracle worker yesterday, today, and forever.

<u>Reflection</u>

1. Think of a time when God came through for you in miraculous fashion. How can reflecting on those times encourage you for the days ahead?

2. If we could collect all the stories from missionaries and saints around the world, we'd likely be stunned by the amount, size, and scope of God's miraculous provision. The majority of what God does will never be known. Spend some time thanking God for His countless miracles around the world.

3. Do you have a specific request for provision? Simple faith moves the heart of God. Believe it today, and when it happens please share it with me and others.

LESSON #18

FIREFLIES

"A dark night lightened up by thousands of glowing fireflies....It's magical."

— ANNA H. VANNIARACHCHY

Beginning in late May, and continuing through mid-July, a unique phenomenon rises each evening from the grass of the Appalachian Mountains. Fireflies, or some would call them lightning bugs, are seen in many places throughout the country. What makes the difference in the mountains of the east is the quantity. I've seen fireflies my whole life, a few here or there, but I've never seen them by the tens of thousands.

Every day we sit at dusk and watch the first flickers of light set against the backdrop of the dark forested mountain behind us. They begin a few feet off the ground, then travel higher to the heights of small trees. As we venture off to sleep, they are swirling around as high as the treetops. Many nights I awake at some point in the night.

Maybe two or three o'clock in the morning. I look outside the window of the camper to see the flickers of light, flickers by the thousands. Some nights we sleep with the curtains pulled back, so we can watch the lights twinkle as we drift off to sleep. It's very hard to capture in a photo with a regular camera, or even a good camera phone. For us, it's something we observe we can only tell people about.

One particular time stands out when we observed this beautiful scene. It was the fourth of July weekend in Shady Valley. If you venture to the mountains, notice the number of firework stands. The good folks of Appalachia love their fireworks, and shoot them off whenever they get a chance. Several houses around Shady Valley have firework shows in their front yards that would rival the ones towns put on in Alabama.

So we decided to head down to the parking lot of a local church in the valley. It gave us a good vantage point of three or four houses that were preparing to shoot hundreds of fireworks. Also, rumor had it, the volunteer fire department was going to have fireworks, and we could see that location from the parking lot as well. As dusk approached we began hearing the boom and crackle of large fireworks being shot. We rolled down our windows, relaxed in the seats, and prepared to see the majestic colors of the bombs. Then we caught a twinkle ahead of us.

There was a field, somewhere in the neighborhood of three acres, just in front of us next to the church. From this field rose clouds, swarms of fireflies. I'm not sure I'd ever seen them this thick at our place. It was as if the whole three acres shimmered with tiny lights dancing up and down. I remember thinking the field looked like a disco ball had been hung over it. For a few minutes we were so transfixed by the fireflies we forgot fireworks were going on all around us. We tried to take pictures to share with our friends back home, but once again it wasn't happening. These fireflies are for memories, you just can't get it in a picture.

So with this backstory I began thinking about the firefly. Such a tiny, insignificant beetle can shine so very brightly in the night. Then I started to think of our own lives. Acts 13:47 says, "For so the Lord has commanded us, saying, "I have made you a light for the Gentiles, that you may bring salvation to the ends of the earth." (ESV) God has made us a light among the people of this earth. We have the responsibility to shine in the darkness. Darkness is simply the absence of light. How do we combat darkness; we shine our light.

If you ever hear my wife tell stories about the trail, she will eventually tell the bear story. We were excited about the lunar eclipse that was happening one night. Our outside light can be turned on, or off, with a switch. Michelle asked me to turn all the lights off, so we could have the best view of the lunar eclipse. The only light near us was our last neighbor up the road. He has a big flood light on his carport, but other than that we were in total darkness at our place. Michelle mentioned she had heard some sticks breaking across the road, but assumed it was likely a raccoon. Suddenly, I heard her scream out, "BIG ANIMAL!" She had caught a glimpse of a huge bear walking across the road in the neighbors light. It walked down into our lot, but we couldn't see it due to the lights being off. We ran for the camper, but tripped over the weedeater I'd left out that afternoon. We were a stumbling mess when we finally got to the camper door. The lesson here, if we'd had light we could have seen the hazards lying unseen in the dark. Likewise, when you shine your light you allow people around you, people you care about, to see hazards and pitfalls. The moment I switched the outside light back on I felt safe. When you fail to shine your light, people around you suffer.

The idea of shining your light comes with a warning. I think about a candle, it can be light, but it can also be hot. For the believer, we need to be sure we shine, but don't burn. I meet people every year on long trails who have stories about hurt caused by a former church, by Christians or people of faith they trusted. I relay it is unfortunate, but their story isn't special. I'm always sympathetic, sometimes apologetic for the hurt they've experienced. I didn't cause the hurt, but I represent what they dislike. I'm willing to be the currier of forgiveness. I do ask you to think about your words, your social media posts, and how we treat others outside of our faith cultures. I've heard people say things like, "The truth hurts." While this is true, the way you convey truth has everything to do with you being perceived as shining over hurting. Perception is commonly viewed as reality.

That little firefly shines bright against the curtain of darkness, but when you have thousands all flashing in unison it is an amazing sight to see. In the same way, we can make a huge difference in the darkness when people of faith come together and shine. This is a reason we love having teams come up to work with us. More people equals more light, more conversations, more love, better understanding. I love seeing groups from multiple congregations come together and show love to their community. The churches in Damascus, VA do an excellent job of this with their Trail Days outreaches to hikers.

A great example was mentioned by Bro. David Strahan recently at a church planting meeting in Alabama. He related a story of a young Robert Louis Stevenson. This lad would grow to become an amazing writer, but he always seemed to have a great grasp of words. One night in the 19th century, he sat at his window transfixed watching men light oil filled lanterns up and down the street. His parents asked him what held his attention so tightly and he replied, "Look, they're punching holes in the darkness."[1]

So what are we doing, we're punching holes in the darkness. Every day when we go out, to the store, the doctors office, your school, or wherever life takes us, we are to let our light shine brightly before each individual we see.

<u>Reflection</u>

1. What are some practical ways you can let your light shine before men?
2. The Bible says not to hide your light. Are there situations (work, sports, family events, get togethers) in life that tempt you to hide your light? How will you handle these situations going forward?
3. Why is unity important for believers who are trying to be a light in a dark world?

LESSON #19

DOING THE RIGHT THING THE WRONG WAY

"Doing the right thing the wrong way is still the wrong thing"

— JAYCE O'NEAL

ountain City, TN is due east of our lot on Hwy 421. We venture over to Mountain City for certain groceries, the hardware store, or if we occasionally don't want to cook. They have an awesome Mexican restaurant there. It is also home to the Johnson County dump; if you read a few of the previous chapters you may have realized I've become a regular taking items to the landfill. Mountain City fancies itself as one of the original homes of country music, and it has murals dedicated to early musicians. It's the county seat of Johnson County, TN and the infamous Copperhead Road, now known as Copperhead Hollow Road, lies just outside town.

On one of my weekly forrays to the Johnson County

dump I noticed something interesting at the main intersection coming into town. There was an older gentleman standing on the corner of the intersection holding a sign. He had parked his truck in the vacant lot very near the road, and placed a sign alongside his truck. I read this sign first, "Turn or burn, repent of your ways ye evildoers." Wow, I was taken off guard. Then I read the sign he carried, it said something to the effect, "Jesus is the only way, repent of your sin now." He carried this sign in one hand and a Bible in the other. He was walking back and forth as if he was in a labor union on strike.

I made my turn, but thought about his tactic as I traveled on to the dump. I admire his courage, it takes a little something to put yourself out there like that. But his message, and the way he went about delivering that message rubbed me the wrong way. Let me give you another example.

Trail Days happens the weekend after Mother's Day in May each year. The town of Damascus, VA has an annual population of around one thousand people give or take. On the weekend of Trail Days the amount of people in town grows to around twenty thousand people. Hikers from all over, near and far, hiking the Appalachian Trail that year or not, come to Damascus. We always participate in the annual outreaches. The churches and town do a great job. Last year we made coffee for hikers after a local church fed them dinner. They had to feed hikers in three rounds because of the volume. Trail Servants, our organization, also does a fruit stand each Friday morning of Trail Days. We give away cups of grapes and strawberries, avocados, kiwis, apples, and bananas. You name a fruit and we are giving it away as hikers walk by. We have fresh water as well. We stop and talk with hikers, give away water, and look for opportunities to pray with them. It's in this atmosphere with vendors, bands, and thousands of hikers that other groups come in.

For the last two years individuals have either sat on the corner with a bullhorn, or walked through the crowds carrying signs saying basically the same as the fellow on the corner. Things like, "Hell is hot and you're headed there," or "Turn from your sin you sinners." Then just walking around with these signs calling people out.

I walked up on this scene last year and saw a few hikers I knew discussing these people.

"Hey Shep, you're who we wanted to see. We were just talking about you. Do you see this?"

"Yes, and I don't like it," I replied.

"That's what I was telling them. I told them this isn't how Shep would do this, this isn't love, this isn't even Christian I doubt."

"No, these people are misguided. Unfortunately, they don't understand half of telling the truth is how you present the truth," I told them.

We left the area and went to grab some food. I later told Michelle I had to fight the fleshly urge to go over and break the guy's sign and throw his bullhorn in Beaverdam Creek. Did he not realize he was doing more to harm the Kingdom's work than help it? See the previous admonishment to shine, not burn. Often people won't remember the words you say, but they will remember how you made them feel. If you made them feel small, unworthy, hated and dirty, how do you think that will go over? If you make people feel invited, loved, a sense of friendship, and let them see the community, then you have an avenue to speak truth.

So you see, sometimes we do the right thing the wrong way. Is it wrong to be bold? Nope. Is it wrong to go to an event and share the gospel? Not at all. Is it wrong to be belligerent, forceful, hateful, and inflammatory? Absolutely.

1 Chronicles 15 tells an interesting story. King David decided it was time to bring the Ark of God to Jerusalem, which was neglected during the reign of Saul. This was definitely the right thing to do. They placed the Ark on an ox cart with Uzzah and Ahio guiding the cart. At a point in the journey the ox stumbled and the Ark rocked causing Uzzah to place his hand on the Ark. This stirred God's anger against him and he was stuck dead. Remember, the Ark was the throne of God in the Old Testament Temple. The place where His presence dwelled. Sinful man cannot come before a Holy God, and He needs no help from man. In this way Uzzah was very wrong to touch the Ark, but this whole matter was David's fault from the beginning.

By placing the Ark on an ox cart David was following the example of the Philistines, not the Word of God. The command of God was clear about moving the Ark. Numbers 4 tells us only the consecrated Levites were to move the Ark. They had to be clean, have proper attire, make sacrifices, and use golden poles which slid into the rings on the Ark. Not even the Levites could just touch the Ark as they pleased. You see it is clear, there is a right way and a wrong way to do things. Sometimes we are doing the right thing, like David, but the wrong way, like David here.

So, when it comes to witnessing to others, I've

mentioned what I feel is the wrong way. Now I'd like to share what I feel is the right way. Recently, I was in a service at Evangel Assembly of God in Montgomery, AL with Pastor Mike Rippy. Pastor Rippy shared with his congregation a simple guide that perfectly describes how we minister, and I will share this with you.

The first step is relationship building. Getting to know someone, building friendship, sharing love. I am very sensitive in this area. People are not projects, I have many folks I have befriended who may never believe like me, and that's okay. They are my friends nonetheless. I am open to sharing with them as the Lord leads, or as they have interest in my faith. This step is of utmost importance.

Secondly, you must be willing to serve people. I guarantee you we have more impact at Trail Days as we serve fruit, and water than the guy with the bullhorn will ever have. We serve hikers up and down the trail. We cook burgers, have fresh fruit, water, sodas, and resupply goods. We give rides, helping those with sprained ankles and busted feet. Our ministry scripture is Mark 9:35, "The first will be last and a SERVANT of all." Serving brings humility, it shows compassion, it is the way Christ would do it.

Next, you have to tell your story. I am not shy when it comes to telling my story. My story of being the redeemed misfit. The troubled college drunk who stumbled into the revival service. Or, the washed up accountant and insurance man who was seeking his true purpose in life. Stories resonate with people. Someone needs to hear your story today. Your story can help lead someone to freedom. Your pain may be the key that opens the lock for another. The key is sharing your story.

Then comes reasoning. I hang out with some of the smartest people. You don't have a clue how much knowledge is walking up and down long trails in America. Make no mistake, that hiker with his thumb out might be the smartest person you've ever met. The issue with all this knowledge is it often comes with a price, that price is being unable to comprehend anything that defies reason. Our God defies reason.

Recently, I was a guest on a hiking podcast. The host holds an advanced degree and was very open and honest. He told me he doesn't really go to church but finds solace in the outdoors. When he is outside there is an element of the unseen in creation, and he can't deny that there could be a divine designer to it all. I mentioned there were some things I believe line up between the Bible and science, but other things must be taken in faith. Ultimately, we must believe in something we can't see. Jesus said blessed is the man that believes and has not seen. You must be able to give an answer for the faith when the time comes.

Lastly, is truth telling. Did the men with the signs tell the truth? They actually did have truthful sayings on the signs. However, they had no relationship with the people. They had not served the hikers. We didn't know their stories; if we had known their stories perhaps we could have related to their methods better. They were unreasonable in their approach. There was no room for discussion, for shared dialog, only screaming into a bullhorn. So the truth they were trying to share was perceived as hateful, it wasn't received at all. [1]

I hope this lesson helps us do the right thing, the right way. Is my way perfect, absolutely not. You may have your own ways, but just remember to let love lead you in every endeavor to reach your neighbor and your community.

Reflection

1. Have you ever been a part of an outreach that had great intentions, but looking back was misguided? What were the long lasting results of this?
2. Reflect on the gospel accounts of Jesus' interactions with hurting people. What can we learn from Christ's approach to ministry?
3. In the five points laid out to help with effective evangelism, what point is hardest for you to apply? What is easiest? How can you work to apply these in your daily life?

LESSON #20
SETTING UP YOUR FOUNDATION

"Get the fundamentals down and the level of everything you do will rise."

— MICHAEL JORDAN

I've previously mentioned my brother, Derek, is my main handyman. He is affectionately known as "Pug" in the area we were raised. Pug and I helped tear down the building that became the bunkhouse, and we began setting up the foundation so we would have it ready when the group arrived from Huntsville. We wanted to be ready when they arrived, so we could go up with the walls.

I am not much of a carpenter. Anyone who knows me will laugh when they read that statement. It's really understated to say not much of a carpenter. God gives people different skills; some have the skills to write books, skills to speak in public, others can build buildings. I got a decent dose of reading, writing, and speaking, but I was allotted not one bit of the building talent. If you see me

126

with a skill saw in my hand you need to take three large steps back.

So we began by working to lay out the area for the bunkhouse, measuring and measuring until we had it right. Then we placed the blocks that would hold the bunkhouse. These had to be precise. The blocks were spaced apart correctly, but the ground was uneven. All the ground in the Appalachian Mountains is uneven; what was I expecting? So we dug, and we measured, we dug, and we placed the level, and we put dirt back, and we measured. Wow! This was turning into a process I wished we could speed up. I became the "level guy." That's the guy who sets the level down and watches the bubble while the other fellow digs and works. We would set sections up, and I'd walk along checking the level.

"What does it look like in the middle," Pug shouted.

"Looks close enough to me," I responded. I was getting tired of the tedious work.

"Let's call it good," I shouted back.

Pug asked me to come measure the very beginning, which I did. Then he asked me how far it was from the center where I had it sitting. I told him, "A little."

"Well, if it's off a little there, it's going to be way off by the time you get to the other end. Just a little up here is a big difference down there. This whole building will be unstable if we don't get this foundation right."

I realized there was a ton of truth in Pug's statement. Truth for the building project we were working on, and truth for our lives in general. We have to get the foundational things correct in our lives, so we have stability to build upon.

I remember hearing a story about the great Green Bay

Packers coach, Vince Lombardi. It was told every year when the Packers reported to start practice he would sit everyone down and pick up a football cleat. He said, "Gentlemen, this is a shoe, this is how you tie your shoe." It was the little things that made the biggest difference, the foundational things.

When I played football we would focus on three things. Blocking, tackling, and running. If you could get those foundational things down you would win ball games. Even in the era of fast paced play with five wide receivers, the team that blocks, tackles and runs better will still win.

To further illustrate Pug's point, I remember an illustration about an airplane. It's called the 1 in 60 rule. Pilots are taught if you are off course by one degree, then you will be 1 mile off course for every 60 miles you fly. If you flew from San Diego, CA to Hawaii and were one degree off course, you would miss the island chain by 42 miles. There are times when this has ended in disaster. In March of 1979 a sightseeing plane crashed in Antarctica because of this. Instead of flying over a lake they flew into a mountain.[1]

This is why it's very important to be careful who you allow to influence your life, specifically in the area of spiritual formation. You are laying a foundation your future growth is dependent upon. It's imperative this foundation is correct, even though we are often tempted to call the process "good enough." It can be painful to allow the Lord to whittle away the wood and level out the ground of our lives. Perhaps in the short term, our lack of maturity, or a bad decision here or there will not hinder us, but in the long term we are undone by this.

As we got more into the project we noticed some of

the bottom boards making up the foundation were rotting. These boards were 2 x 8's. We decided to remove anything with water damage or rot, and replace the foundation 2 x 8's with 2 x 10's. This would make it safer, and make it stronger. We were moving the building from a lower elevation with less snow load, to a higher elevation with more chance of snow. We needed to be sure it would hold the load.

A good foundation in your life affects you, but it also affects those who depend on you. Your children, friends, and your decisions can all be affected. Perhaps you have some rot in your foundation, some things you know need to go. It's not too late to do some Holy Spirit inspired maintenance. Ask God to illuminate those rotting places, and rebuild the foundations. We do this with proper spiritual discipline.

Just like blocking, tackling, and running are the building blocks of a good ball team, Scripture reading, prayer, and worship are foundational to our walk with the Lord. These are foundational. Time spent with Jesus, in His presence, can't be replaced with anything else. Our daily, personal devotional life keeps the rot at bay.

Early in my process of becoming a US Missions Missionary Chaplain I asked my advisor what was the difference in success and failure. What did she see as the greatest pitfall for someone like me? Her response was instantaneous. Lack of personal devotional time with the Lord. She stated any minister that failed to make it, moral failure or otherwise, shared one trait. They became slack in their daily Scripture reading, prayer, and worship.

The good news is it's not too late to secure your foundation. If you are older and reading this, know you can inspect and repair what may have been damaged by neglect and wear. If you are younger, you are like Pug and I, setting the foundation at a pivotal point in your life. Make sure you are placing it on the firm bedrock of a relationship with Christ. In the shortsighted near future it may not seem to be that important, but give it time. One day you will look back and be thankful you got the foundation right.

<u>Reflection</u>

1. In what ways can we check our lives to be sure they are staying "on center?"
2. I challenge you to ask the Lord to do a foundation inspection. Be sure you have the stability to handle the load God wants you to carry.
3. I gave you a few spiritual disciplines (prayer, Bible reading, worship), but this is not an exhaustive list. What are other disciplines you find useful in your daily devotional time?

LESSON #21

WE'RE ALL IN THIS TOGETHER

"Alone we can do so little; together we can do so much."

— HELEN KELLER

The following story was given to me second hand, but it was told for the truth, based on actual events so to say. I was at a hostel and the owner was telling me about a close knit group of hikers from the previous hiking season. She said they were the tightest trail family she'd ever seen. If one person had to stop for a day or two, they all stopped. They had a bond. I inquired as to why she thought their bond was so special, and this is the story she told.

She said they were a southbound group; they had started really early in the season. Southbound means they went from Maine to Georgia, not Georgia to Maine. Most people will tell you southbound is harder in some ways, perhaps more dangerous. The reasoning makes sense. You are tackling the harder states of Maine and New Hampshire first. There are difficult water crossings, you have the 100 mile wilderness, and hike above treeline in New Hampshire. Northbound hikers have over a thousand miles of hiking to prepare for these challenges. Southbound hikers start with these challenges.

With starting early, there was still a chance of snow in the northeast. Sure enough, at some point in New Hampshire, they got dumped on. A foot or more of snow came down, this was not hiking for the faint of heart. They packed their frozen tents and started hiking the first day. They walked in line, one behind the other. It was quickly determined the hiker in front was doing all the work breaking the snow. This made it easier for those walking behind. They devised a plan, each one would take turns rotating to the front. This way would keep a fresh person out front, and then that hiker would rotate to the easiest spot in the back. This was the pattern they followed for a couple days. Working together very possibly saved one another's lives. Going through this harrowing time together made them extremely close.

There is great power in partnership. In 1 Corinthians 3:6 Paul tells the church, "I planted, Apollos watered,but God gave the increase." What he is describing is partnership. Everyone is doing their part. One is called to water, one is called to plant, we all do our part. This is why the body of believers need one another.

I have people ask from time to time how I feel about formal church. I tell them I love the local church, I'm a product of it. Yes, I feel the presence of the Lord at a waterfall, but that doesn't take the place of the corporate body of believers. I'm blessed to have a church family who prays for me. I need these people.

Recently, I spoke at a church and used the example of the fireplace app on my television. This app, or channel, brings up what appears to be a beautiful fireplace. When you first start watching it is brand new wood. As you watch the wood burn down, more fresh wood is added, just like a real campfire. It looks so real you are half tempted to grab some marshmallows and attempt to roast them, but it's not real. You don't feel the heat from the fire. You won't walk away smelling like smoke. It's an illusion, it'll do in a pinch. It's nice to turn the fireplace app on while it's raining outside and I can't build a real one.

I don't have anything against church on the internet. It'll do in a pinch, it's good when you're sick and can't get out. Or, perhaps you're stuck on the side of a mountain on a Wednesday night. It's great for catching a good word online in these situations, but you don't feel the heat from the fire exactly the same. You need other people. God created us to exist in community.

Technology seems to keep us better connected. The problem is it connects us in a very impersonal way. I can shoot my friends a quick message, reply to their insta-gram story, or send an email. This still doesn't take the place of sitting down with friends and enjoying conversa-tion around the dinner table. I know I may sound old fashioned, but I'm worried ensuing generations may lose the ability to function in social settings. Zoom meetings are great, but they'll never be exactly the same as sitting around the conference room. I remember being young going to a friend's house and meeting their parents. Shaking their father's hand, hugging their mom. We can't do this when our whole connection is virtual. Social media does not teach social skills. You can have five thousand "friends" on Facebook and still be a very lonely person.

I've met people who have hiked for miles alone. They will tell you being solitary for long periods of time seems to have a negative effect on them. I personally need to go out and just be alone occasionally. The key word is occasionally, and not for prolonged periods. Your mind starts to play tricks on you when you are alone for too long.

Way back when I dispatched flatbed trucks we used to call it "windshield time." It's when a driver was on a long haul and had days of driving just looking at the windshield all alone. These drivers would call in, having turned every molehill in their mind into a mountain. They would have concocted theories on everything from the payscale to the vending machines in the terminal lobby. All because they lacked personal interaction in their day to day lives. The mind is a tricky thing, and nobody is immune.

The lot in Shady Valley could be a lonely place if we allowed it to be. We are at the top of a valley, three thousand feet above sea level. Our closest permanent neighbor passed away tragically last summer. I do like the solitary nature of the place, but I'm a social creature by design. So, Michelle and I are always heading to town, to the dollar store, to the swimming hole with the kids, or to church. Whatever we can do to get more social interaction, because we know it's good for the soul.

The Canadian Mental Health Association (CMHA) has a great article on the importance of human connection. It states by neglecting interaction and connection, we put our health at risk. There is a greater risk of depression and anxiety when we lack connection. On the other hand, when we engage with others we improve our immune systems, have better regulated emotions, and higher self esteem. Here are some things to consider if you're feeling disconnected according to the CMHA:

- Joining a new club or group
- Reaching out to old friends
- Find a cause you care about and volunteer
- Eat lunch in an open area with other people
- Find neighbors you don't know and introduce yourself
- Do random acts of kindness
- Ask someone for help if you need it[1]

These are practical ways to find community. For the believer, it is important to find a community of believers to join. I hear the objections all the time. "I didn't like the music there. I didn't like the sermon. My third grade teacher was mean and she goes to that church. There are hypocrites there." The fact is we can find an excuse to do, or not to do just about anything. There is no perfect church, no perfect place of worship, no perfect pastor or leadership, and no perfect members. I've attended churches from one end of this country to another. From Alabama all the way up into New England. We've visited multiple denominations. I can verify, there is no perfect place. People are people everywhere you go. Even though some of these excuses have validity, the fact I need people around me, standing in the gap for me, interceding for me, is more important than any excuse.

The enemy is a master excuse maker. He wants you to operate in solitude. 1 Peter describes him as a roaring lion seeking whom he may devour. Lions don't go blazing into the herd full speed. They know the herd has more numbers than them, and might fight against them. Lions wait until a member falls away from the herd. They watch to see if one gets separated, then they attack. We need the herd. We are better together. Don't fight alone. We're all in this together.

Reflection

1. Can you think of a time when you needed the help of others? How did it feel knowing you had a community around you willing to help?
2. Have you ever experienced "windshield time?" A time when you've had too much alone to think and blow everything out of proportion.
3. Reflect on how the community was built 40 years ago, or even 20 years ago. When people visited on porches, and didn't have phones in their pockets. How can we ensure future generations understand the importance of true community?

LESSON #22
REFURBISHED

"Even in the best of worlds the soul needs refurbishing from time to time."

— CLARISSA PINKOLA ESTES

I get the chance to hang out with some of the most creative people in the world. I love creativity, even though it's not a strong point of mine. I'm the guy that sees the way you turned an old wash pot into a new plant stand, and buys the plant stand because it's so awesome. Then I always think how great it would have been if I'd thought of that.

The people around me are always refurbishing things. Refurbishing means to renovate, repair, or make something completely new from an old item. Old barrels, truck tailgates, window frames, you name it, I've seen something amazing come from it.

Recently, I traveled up to Beckley, West Virginia. Aside from the roads, which made me incredibly carsick, I loved

West Virginia. This was one of my first forays into the heart of the state. The Appalachian Trail goes through the eastern panhandle of West Virginia, only touching around four miles of the state. I'd spent more time in this area, near Harpers Ferry. It's not the same as the central part of the state. If you ever get a chance to go to West Virginia, you should take it. The newest National Park in the country is there, it's a great spot for history lovers, and the people are some of the finest folks you'll ever meet. Just make sure you know how to properly say Appalachia (Appa-latch-uh).

Typically when I'm in a new area I look for a coffee shop to work in. I've written more than half this book in coffee shops from Florida to West Virginia. I didn't even like coffee until I started writing. When I needed a place to work I'd just go in and get the cheapest coffee. It's bad manners to sit in a place, use their electricity and wi-fi, and not order something.

The cheapest coffee is just plain black with a little cream and sugar. That's what I go with, straight coffee, or cold brew, one cream, one sugar. It makes me feel like a sophisticated fellow with my, almost black, coffee while everyone else has their dainty frappuccino with whipped toppings. They don't realize I'm trying to find the cheapest way to buy myself a place to write for three hours.

I found the Hilltop Coffee Company in Beckley. It's a cool little spot in an old school. The building was literally a refurbished project. The old school had been bought and turned into a doctor's building. The part not used as a doctor's building was converted into Hilltop Coffee Company.

As I settled in to write I noticed the interesting looking boards on the wall in front of me. I thought it was a really cool look, they'd used some type of boarding to cover this whole wall. I'm a fan of accent walls, using old pallet wood for walls, and generally anything you can do to reuse old wood. When my friend arrived he mentioned the wall.

In a cool twist the wood on the wall was made using the old wooden bleachers from the school. What an amazing idea! Such a neat way to use materials on hand, and keep some of the history from the school. I began to think of the basketball games played in this space. The feet that walked up and down the bleachers, parents cheering for their kids, teenagers encouraging their friends. The children that sat on the steps and did homework, and the delinquents that gathered underneath. There's lots of history in a place like this.

Many hostels near the Appalachian Trail use old, leftover materials as a way to preserve history, and save money. Many outdoor showers have repurposed doors, old windows used in unique ways, and wood from barns torn down many years ago. Even our bunkhouse is a refurbished backyard shed.

It's interesting Matthew 13:55 mentions Jesus as the carpenter's son. From what we know about trades those days we make the assumption Jesus would have learned this skill from His father, and He himself would have been a carpenter. Building and repair work were the main functions of carpenters in this time. We don't know much about the life of Christ prior to the events recorded in the Gospels, but we can be reasonably certain Jesus engaged in the family trade for a time. He would have been a man who worked with His hands to repair the broken legs of a stool. Perhaps He sanded and smoothed the rough edges away from chairs or tables. Maybe He found old broken pieces of wood and fashioned them together to create a new item.

When you think about it, the Lord is a master at using refurbished materials. Every believer was once an old, broken vessel. 2 Corinthians 5:17 says, "If anyone is in Christ they are a new creation. The old has passed away, and the new has come." Our old purpose is gone, and we have a new, exciting purpose. The old stuff that used to define us (brokenness, sin, failure) is replaced by the new things that now define us (peace, grace, forgiveness, salvation).

In my own life I have had rough edges made smooth over time by the hand of the Master Carpenter. I have been broken, rebuilt, and repurposed. Many times I've thought I was done, headed for the corner, the yardsale, or the dump. Only to have the Master pick me up, tighten a few pegs, replace a few boards, level me, and make me new.

One of the greatest examples of God refurbishing a life is found in the story of Rahab. In Joshua chapter 2 we are introduced to a woman known as Rahab the Harlot, or Prostitute. We know she hid the spies, and was spared in the destruction of Jericho because of this. She then married into a Jewish family, but not just any Jewish family. Matthew 1:5 tells us she married Salmon of the tribe of Judah, and was the mother of Boaz. Boaz was the father of Obed, Obed fathered Jesse, and Jesse was the father of David. Yep, that Shepherd boy who slew a giant and became King of Israel. So Rahab the Harlot became the great-great-great grandmother of King David. We know Jesus would ultimately come from this lineage. What a transformation. There are many restoration projects in Scripture, but perhaps none more dramatic than the story of Rahab the Prostitute, who became Rahab the Grandmother of Jesus.

If you are wondering about purpose, perhaps thinking your time has passed, place your trust in the Divine Refurbisher. Allow the Lord to firm up your life, sand down the rough patches, and return you to usefulness. Throughout the centuries there are countless stories of God taking the least, the last, and the left behind, and using them for His glory. Let the Master Carpenter restore any broken thing in you.

Reflection

1. How does the image of Christ as a Master Carpenter shed new light on 2 Corinthians 5:17?
2. Think of a time you've experienced the refurbishing/repurposing power of God.
3. Give a few Biblical examples that show the refurbishing power of God. (There are more than I can mention in this book)

LESSON #23

WOULDA SHOULDA COULDA FOREST

"We crucify ourselves between two thieves: regret for yesterday and fear of tomorrow."

— FULTON OURSLER

When we ventured out to serve as missionaries we decided the only way to fulfill our call was to homeschool the kids. We have loved our homeschool journey. The kids get that question often. "How do you guys like school?" They really love it.

I enjoy the chance to teach them about things I love, like history. Once, as we were working on the lot, Meredith asked, "Where is the land the Native Americans were moved from?" She was appalled when I told her she was standing on that land. Meredith is a lover of animals and underdogs. In many ways she is my most compassionate child, though only people close to her know this. Her question gave us a great opportunity to explore the topic of the Cherokee National Forest, which surrounds our property.

Overall, the Appalachian Trail passes through fourteen states, six national parks, and eight national forests. The national forests contain about 47% of the trail. The Cherokee National Forest is one forest the trail traverses. Typically, when I say Cherokee National Forest, people think of the town near Great Smoky Mountains National Park. This is not the same place. The Cherokee National Forest is in two parts, a northern area and a southern area. These two areas are divided by the Great Smoky Mountains National Park. Our lot is in the northern area, 139 miles north of Cherokee, NC.

These national forests are treasures, filled with things to see, do, and enjoy. Many have hiking trails that bring in tourists. The Cherokee National Forest has over seven hundred miles of hiking trails, the Appalachian Trail being 150 of those miles. Even though hikers are surrounded by the beauty of these national forests, there are times when another forest can consume the mind. I call it the Woulda Shoulda Coulda Forest.

The Woulda Coulda Shoulda Forest is the forest of regret. For some people regret is a crippling emotion. Daniel Pink has authored studies on regret and his findings are interesting. He found regret is the second most prevalent emotion listed on his surveys after love. Also, nearly 20% of respondents admit dealing with regret all the time. After looking at statistics from around the globe, Pink says there are four foundational categories of regret.

The first are foundational regrets. These regrets have long term implications for your life. Choices to neglect school, or neglect your health long term. I can say for certain I regret my performance in junior high school. I was a horrible student, I didn't have a care in the world, and I hated math. Rather than make myself better, study hard, and learn, I skated through. I barely tried when it came to math class. I'm still not sure how I passed at all. As an adult that homeschools his children I'm thankful for the teaching DVDs. There is nothing I can tell my kids that will help them in math. We've had to shell out hundreds of dollars through the years for math tutors because I don't have a clue. I often think, "What if I'd tried a little in Doc's math class, I could of saved that money."

The next type identified by Pink are boldness regrets. These involve a once in a lifetime opportunity that requires bold action. Do you take the step? Did you ask the pretty girl to dance? Or spiritually, did you obey the Lord and go on that mission trip? I remember an old shirt from the 90s that boldly said, "YOU MISS 100% OF THE SHOTS YOU DON'T TAKE." Do not be afraid to take bold action in your life, and remember life favors the bold.

The third type are moral regrets. Unfortunately, as a minister, I have encountered people dealing with these regrets more often than not. People we've hurt through our own moral shortcomings. Relationships forever scarred by unfaithfulness. Moral regrets are centered on other people and how we've treated them. Over the past twenty years I've gone back and apologized to many people as the Lord has led me. People I hurt when I was a drunk. Kids I bullied around too much in high school. Without fail those individuals have always been gracious, most have forgotten the offense, but it was something I regretted.

The last type is perhaps the most common, and they're connection regrets. This involves lost relationships with family, friends, or acquaintances through neglect. We may not think about this one often, but we're most likely all guilty here. I have made it a life mission to get better and better at staying connected with friends. You must be very intentional with this, but it's so worth it. My old friends I still see from time to time are treasures of my life. Even if it's just a text, or a quick call, I always love it. I'm nostalgic by nature. I do regret some relationships that have faltered, but I'm immensely happy I do have some twenty and thirty year friends today.[1]

In Lesson 10 of my previous book I mention Paul's words from Phillipians chapter 3. The words that jump from the Bible is the phrase "forgetting those things which are behind." Remember, Paul had some stuff in his closet. He'd consented to the stoning of Stephen, imprisoned Chirstians, and actively fought against early Christianity. Those are items worth regretting, but he also knew wallowing in that regret does nothing for our future.

Regret is like a ball and chain tied around your ankle, it slows you down and wears you out. Paul basically says, "The beauty of what's ahead of me is so amazing it overtakes everything behind me in my past." The Woulda Shoulda Coulda Forest will overtake us if we let it, but God will remove that pain we carry if we let Him.

When I allowed the Lord to restore my life around 2004 I remember one song did more for me than any other. I'm going to show my age with this one, but "Ocean Floor" by Audio Adrenaline dealt with regret of past sins and transgressions. The song is based on Psalm 103:12, "As far as the east is from the west, so far does He remove our transgressions from us." (ESV) I had to pull the car over a couple times overwhelmed with emotion listening to that one back then. If you want to find a way out of the Woulda Shoulda Coulda Forest, find some good music that ministers to your soul, and start praising your way out.

Learn scripture. Another key to escaping the forest of regret is Scripture. I once had sticky notes with Scripture stuck all along the bottom edge of my work computer. Jesus used Scripture to combat the enemy; why do we think we can do it without Scripture?

Reconnect with friends who are beneficial to your life. Notice I said, "beneficial." Some folks are still stuck in the same rut they were in twenty years ago, those are not the folks to reconnect with. Perhaps you had a pastor or ministry leader who was influential to your life and you've lost contact. Look them up. I can attest it does a minister's heart good to hear someone they worked with twenty years ago tell them what an impact they've had. It could have been a friend, or a teacher, maybe a coach you regret losing contact with.

I recently reconnected with a teacher/coach of mine from 25 years ago. First, I apologized for being a horrible student in 8th grade. It was very cool to see how much each of us had grown. It's never too late to reconnect.

The Woulda Shoulda Coulda Forest can be a doozy to navigate. For those overwhelmed by regret it is something that will take the Lord to overcome. When people say things like, "I've been so bad, how can God love me, or use me?" I ask, "How many Chirstians have you killed, or locked in prison?" Typically, "None" is the response. I reply, "Well the guy that did that wrote ⅔ of the New Testament, so don't beat yourself up too bad."

<u>**Reflection**</u>

1. Look up a few Scriptures that deal with regret. What is God saying to you through these verses?
2. I've heard several people speak of songs/hymns the Lord used to unlock their chains of regret and pain. I told you one of mine, what is one of yours?
3. How does focusing on the upward, forward call of Christ free you from the past?

LESSON #24
WEEPING MAY ENDURE FOR THE NIGHT

"Every Problem Has An Expiration Date"

— UNKNOWN

All hikers have trail names. These are bestowed upon you in much the same manner as nicknames. Usually it's something that happens to you, something you said, or a natural trait. A couple years back we knew of a hiker with the trail name Chris Rock. He looked just like the comedian, Chris Rock. My trail name is Shep, short for Shepherd, and Michelle's trail name is No Miles. If you ask around the trail for Brad and Michelle you may get blank stares, but mention Shep and No Miles and people know who you're talking about. One of the more unique trail names in our family is Footloose.

Footloose is Lane's trail name. He earned this name due to his laid back, clumsy nature. When he hikes he isn't as mindful of roots and rocks as he should be. He trips so often it looks like he is dancing down the trail. When

Lane knocked himself unconscious in Pennsylvania, the ambulance driver asked him what his trail name was. When he replied, "Footloose" the driver said, "Well you've earned that name today, buddy." It's good practice to know where Lane is when trekking a difficult, dangerous part of the trail. You don't want the person at the rear falling and taking the whole group out.

Last summer, Lane managed to string together an improbable list of injuries. First, he severely sprained his ankle in Tennessee, which put him in a walking boot for two weeks. He got out of the boot for a week and twisted it again - right back to the walking boot. Then, he went to his first basketball practice of the year and tore his ACL. In his defense, the doctor said these injuries can be common with teens who grow too fast. Being somewhat injury prone can be a side effect.

It was after Lane's ACL surgery he dropped wisdom on me that became the inspiration for this lesson. About two weeks after surgery, and after a day of intense physical therapy, I came home to find Lane with his leg propped up resting. I asked about therapy, and he replied in his normal teenage way, "Good." Then, I asked him if it was painful. I asked if he shed any tears. He said, "Dad, sometimes you go through things in life, and even though you know it's going to be better, you still got to cry."

Psalm 30:5 says, "Weeping may endure for the night, but joy comes in the morning." This verse serves as a constant reminder no matter what you may be going through currently, eventually you will experience joy again. Even in the darkest night we know the sun will rise again. What if we're going through a season that looks as if it will lead to death?

It's hard to have joy in the middle of a diagnosis, or painful life event. However, I hear the words of Job chapter 19 when he says, "But as for me, I know that my redeemer lives, and He will stand upon the earth at last. And after my body has decayed, yet in my body I will see God! I will see Him for myself. Yes, I will see Him with my own eyes. I am overwhelmed at the thought." (NLT) Job said even if his sorrow was unto death, he would stand before God in the end. For the believer, even the worst case scenario, the worst possible diagnosis, the most feared outcome, still leads to joy in the morning. It still leads to eternal life. Like the old hymnist said, "If I go or if I stay, I'm a winner either way."

Here's another key. When Lane was injured I was amazed at how well he took the news. Kids preparing for their junior season of sports typically see losing that season as a horrible blow. I was prepared to have to really talk to him about what was important in life. I figured he'd be down in the dumps, but he wasn't. Shockingly, he handled the injury with much more maturity than his dad would have at sixteen. The key is this, our attitude helps determine how long the night of weeping lasts.

You see, joy does not come from lack of trouble. A person pursues happiness, but chooses joy. Joy is an inner feeling that endures through hardship. That positive attitude goes hand in hand with joy. The trial doesn't have to end for the morning to come. The morning comes when we allow the joy of the Lord to transform us regardless of our external circumstances. The joy of the Lord is our strength.

I asked Lane's physical therapist how much attitude and joy affected the overall recovery time for patients. She said it was somewhere in the neighborhood of 60-70%. So choosing joy shortens the night of weeping, and it physically shortens the recovery time in some cases. Then she said something interesting. Trust also affects healing time.

I thought about that for a minute. Many times we allow the dark night of weeping to continue, because we haven't fully trusted the Lord in our situation. I am no different than anyone else. In my flesh I am prone to bouts of fear, frustration, and panic when things don't go my way. I trust in my own reasoning of the situation too much. Proverbs 28:26 says, "Those who trust in their own reasoning are fools, but those who walk in wisdom will be kept safe." The hard thing for me to do is not trust myself, but my reasoning is flawed. So what does walking in wisdom look like, and how does it lead to joy?

James 3:15-17 tells us there are two types of wisdom. You have earthly wisdom, and Heavenly wisdom. Human, earthly wisdom is unspiritual, self help type stuff. I will occasionally read some of these books, but there are depths of despair this type of wisdom can't help you with. Heavenly wisdom is Bible based, Christ centered, and Spirit led. As my old friend Bro. Hoagie Adamson used to say, "Bro. Brad, we got to be Spirit fed and Spirit led."

So, joy comes from the Lord. It comes from a good attitude, from trusting the Lord, and walking in wisdom. In this life we will have trouble, it's guaranteed, it's a red letter statement, Jesus said it. Then He said this, "But be of good cheer, for I have overcome the world." I find lots of comfort in this statement. Sometimes we have to cry, weeping may endure for a night, but be of good cheer, because JOY comes in the morning.

<u>Reflection</u>

1. Explain in your own words the difference between joy and happiness.
2. Reflect on a time when you had to choose joy even in the midst of a difficult season. How did God grow you in that season?
3. At the first sign of trouble, are you tempted to lean on earthly wisdom? Why is understanding heavenly wisdom important to our reactions in painful seasons?

LESSON #25
RAFTING RULES

"When all else fails, follow directions."

— ANNE LAMOTT

I've been rafting on several rivers in the Appalachian Mountains. We really enjoy rafting trips, and when groups come to work with us they sometimes choose rafting as their free day excursion. If you've never been rafting I will try and describe some aspects of a trip so you understand this lesson. First, you get to the company shop and sign your group up. Then you will be assigned a guide. Raft guides are some of the most unique people you will meet in the outdoor community. Hilarity is part of the job description, they have to be part adventure athlete, part standup comedian. The guides are nearly always very chill, personable, and incredibly knowledgeable about the rivers they guide.

After the guide assignment you will be grouped together by boat crews with your guide, get your equipment, and board the bus to ride over to the put in location. This bus ride is crowded, and I feel carsick as we travel the winding mountain roads. On this ride one of the guides will stand up near the front and go over a series of rules. These rules are there for your protection on the river, and they closely relate to walking with the Lord.

The main gist of the rules is, "Help the raft guides, help you." You play an active part in your rescue if something happens on the river. The most effective form of rescue is self rescue. The first thing you must do is follow directions.

You get lots of important directions for safety from the guides. If you fall overboard you are to follow the nose and toes rule. You have a life jacket on, so lean your head back, which keeps your face above water, and float with your feet up. The reason you must keep your feet up is because there are old trees and rocks below the surface which can snag you and hold you under water. The nose and toes rule is very important. Then you need to look for the rope the guide will throw you. It may not land directly on you, so you may have to paddle towards the rope, you play a part in the rescue. Finally, when you get close to the boat the guide will grab the top of the life vest, and you will need to help launch yourself up as they pull you back into the boat.

Another aspect of direction following is your paddling cadence. You normally have six or eight people in the raft plus your guide. You are divided evenly on both sides of the boat, and the guide sits at the back. The guide will call out the strokes, and everyone must listen and paddle together. He might say, "Right side two," which is two paddle strokes for one side and none for the other. Then he could say, "everyone three," which is the whole boat doing three strokes together. You have to pay close atten-tion to the directions because failing to follow these instructions could send you into a rock, or get you stuck in a precarious waterflow which dumps the whole boat. The guides know the river, they know exactly where you need to go for success, they will take you there but you must listen and follow directions.

In the Christian walk we are given a clear set of direc-tions. We have the Word of God and the indwelling Holy Spirit. Both work together to guide the life of a believer. We should not think we know better than God. If we attempt to navigate life's troubled waters without God's guidance, we run the risk of encountering dangerous situa-tions we could have avoided. So many times in my life I've smashed against the proverbial rock. I've failed to listen and found myself in turbulent waters. When we fail to follow directions we put ourselves and others in unneeded peril.

I've made this point, but it bears repeating. The people you allow in your raft can make or break you. In a raft, if you have one or two people who don't listen, their actions could put you in danger because they're in your boat. The people you associate with, surround yourself with, and have in your crew can be your undoing. It's a tale as old as time, but people fall victim to this pitfall everyday. Make sure you have good people in the boat with you!

The second important rafting instruction is don't panic. You won't remember the directions you were given about your nose and toes if you fall overboard and go full panic mode. I've seen this happen. Someone goes over and they come up thrashing all about, their mouth is open gulping water, hands waving wildly, feet dragging in the water underneath. Panic leads to forgetting our directions, often doing the exact opposite of what we've been told to do.

Now think about our lives. We get a bad scan, and we panic. Our heat pump goes out, and we panic. The kids are having trouble in school, and we react in fear and panic. Believe me, this is the song leader talking to the choir. I have reacted to situations with fear and panic more times than faith. I hate to say that. I'm thankful the Lord has taught me differently these last few years, but it's been a process.

Recently, I drove up to West Virginia in our Toyota Highlander. There is no good way to travel in the mountains, it puts stress on vehicles, there is no getting around it. I know one trail angel on the Appalachian Trail who has had several transmissions replaced over the years in her van. The mountains are a grind. Sure enough, at the end of my trip the Highlander started making a crazy noise. Old Brad would have immediately panicked, thrown his hands in the air, said goodbye to any savings, and hit the Chinese buffet to eat his cares away. Surely the transmission was shot. I didn't do that. I told Michelle we'd get it looked at, whatever was wrong the Lord would make a way. I didn't stress over it for a minute. We took it to the shop and sure enough it was fine. There was nothing worth panicking over. When we panic, just like we mentioned with fear, we rob ourselves of today's peace by getting all worked up over a situation that likely is fine.

Paul was a man who didn't panic. He was shipwrecked, snakebit, beaten, but not panicked. In Philippians 4:6 he writes these words, "Do not be anxious about anything, but in everything by prayer and supplication with thanksgiving let your requests be made known to God." (NIV) He was possibly chained to a house arrest guard at the time he wrote the words "don't panic over anything."

The final bit of instruction from the guide was trust your guide. You had to trust your guide had the knowledge to get you from point A to point B safely. If you didn't trust him you were unlikely to obey his instructions. My favorite verse on trusting the Lord is Proverbs 3:5-6. It says, "Trust in the Lord with all your heart, and lean not on your own understanding; In all your ways acknowledge Him, and He will direct your paths." (NKJV) The lean not on your own understanding is crucial.

I have a funny rafting story. It's actually my earliest rafting story, and involves a family vacation. When I was in about eighth grade we took a vacation to the mountains. This would have put my brother Pug around fifth grade, and my sister Mandy in tenth grade. Our family decided we wanted to go rafting, and for some reason our parents decided this could be undertaken without a raft guide. At the time I saw nothing wrong with this picture. Other people have guides at the back of the boat directing, we had my dad, Mack. After all, the guides do this for a living, and we are on a one off trip. What's the worst that could happen? I should probably ask Mom and Dad why we decided to do it this way, but if I had to guess it was to save money. If you've ever taken a family of five to Gatlinburg you understand the logic.

I really only remember two things about that trip. We got a ton of water in the boat, and we had to periodically stop to flip the water from the boat. I've never done this on any other rafting trips, so I think this goes back to leaning on our own understanding of rafting. On one occasion, when we stopped to flip the water we were just short of the bank. My brother volunteered to jump out of the boat and pull us to the bank. The water only looked to be maybe six inches deep. Pug went completely under and never touched the bottom. I had to pull him back into the boat. This water was so clear it looked shallow but was actually very deep.

The other memory is the end of the trip. I could do without this memory. The guides do a good job of preparing you for tricky falls and drops in the river. They explain what's coming up ahead, how you need to paddle, and how to lock your feet under the seat in front of you so you don't fly around. Well, we didn't have a guide. The last feature of the trip was a class 3 rapid with a small waterfall. All I remember is three or four of us ended up piled on top of one another upside down in the bottom of the boat. Lean not on your own understanding.

Listen to directions, don't panic, and trust your guide. These are rules for rafting, but your life is immensely better when we apply them to our spiritual walk as well. If you do these things everyone gets to their destination safely.

Reflection

1. Of the three rules for rafting, which do you find to be the hardest for you to follow?
2. Think about the people in your boat. The people you allow in your inner circle, close friends, work buddies, people you have over to your house. Are these folks encouraging or discouraging to your Christian walk? What are the consequences of having the wrong people in your life?
3. I described our family trip. Has there been a time you leaned on your own understanding and came up short? What lessons did you learn about trusting the Lord to direct your paths?

LESSON #26
THE ROOT

"When solving problems, dig at the roots instead of just hacking at the leaves."

— ANTHONY D'ANGELO

The grass is lush during the spring and summer seasons at the lot in Shady Valley. We have ample rain throughout this time. The lower Appalachia area is basically a rainforest. Everything grows well in this area. The problem is everything can include lots of weeds.

When we first started the work at the lot we couldn't cut the grass with a push mower, it was far too overgrown. We had to weedeat the grass and uncover the many river rocks strewn throughout the yard. We finally got to the point of mowing the lot, and the next issue was the weeds. You can mow them down, but they will grow right back. No matter how many times you try, you will never remove a weed with a lawnmower. The cutting is only temporary.

The lawn looks great immediately after cutting, the weeds appear just like grass, but this is only a surface level fix. Give it two weeks and the weeds are back, lush, bigger and better than ever. The best way to fix the problem long term is to go through the yard and pull the weeds up from the roots.

I had a couple stay with me for a few days. They enjoyed relaxing on the lot, and spent part of one day weeding a rough section. I told them this wasn't a work for stay situation, but they enjoyed gardening and saw it more as stress relief. It was nice to recapture that area of ground. The key is, you can't just cut the surface, you must get the roots.

In our own lives we face the same challenge. Many of us are struggling and we continue struggling because we treat the symptoms and not the problem. Take a runny nose. I've been sick before and tried to treat the symptoms. You'd take something for the cough, the runny nose, the red eyes, and any other issue you might have. The underlying issue may be you have the flu, but you never treat the flu, you treat the symptoms. This allows the flu to rage until you get the medicine that actually treats the flu. It's the same as cutting the grass vs. pulling the weeds. You have to fix the underlying problem. Only dealing with surface level issues will result in temporary results.

Too often we are satisfied with limited victory when God desires us to have total victory. In 2 Kings 13 we find the story of Elisha nearing death. The king visits and inquires about the enemies of Israel. Elisha tells him to shoot an arrow out the window. So he shot the arrow of the Lord's deliverance out the window towards Syria. Next, Elisha tells him to smite the ground with the remaining arrows. The king hit the ground three times and stopped. This upset the prophet. He told the king he limited God by hitting the ground only three times, he wouldn't get complete victory. The goal is total victory.

If the root causes aren't dealt with we will never get total victory. For instance, take a drug addict. On the surface the problem seems to be drugs. If the addict could just get clean from the drugs... However, I've found most addicts are using drugs to dull the pain of a much deeper trauma in their lives. For some it's abuse or neglect from childhood. Others come from marginalized communities and broken homes. There are so many deeper factors than drug abuse. Those deeper issues are the places we must go to see true freedom. Don't just cut the grass, get the roots.

If we don't deal with the root causes, then the problems grow and intensify. When Israel first crossed into the Promised Land, God told them not to allow any enemies to survive. They were not to allow any enemies to remain. Joshua 11:22 tells us three Philistine cities were allowed to remain, the cities of Gaza, Gath, and Ashdod. Years later Gath is listed as the home of the Philistine champion Goliath. What you don't deal with today could become a giant tomorrow.

Dealing with things on the surface is easy, getting to the root cause is hard. Anyone that has ever pulled up shrubbery, or attempted to tame a mimosa bush knows the struggle. You can trim it down easily. It doesn't take too much work to cut them even with the ground. The true work comes when you deal with what you don't see, the part below the surface. You have to dig, and chop, and dig, and hook a chain up to the back of a tractor, and finally you get the root system removed. It's an arduous process to get the whole root system up, but that's what you must do to totally remove the plant and keep it from coming back.

It's the same with us. It's very easy to work on what you see. When you see an alcoholic you see the drink in his hand. We know someone with crippling anxiety who can't leave the house. Surface level solutions are easy solutions. The true fix for what ails us is found much deeper. The work to be done is harder, and is more personal.

There was a time in my life when I was prone to bouts of anger. I'd get mad and just fly off the handle. I sat down and asked myself the question, "What is the root cause of this problem?" The answer for me was a couple things. First, I come from a long line of tough people. I mentioned Elamville in a previous chapter. It was a tough place, full of rough people. These were my people, my relatives. I'm proud of where I came from, but I realize some of my issues come through these genetics. We may be predisposed to certain issues. We have to understand our acceptance of Christ is a new birth, we are a new creation, we are not bound by the former dispositions of our old nature. Claim these promises and rely on them.

I also came to understand my quick trigger anger was a survival response of sorts. I grew up a poor, overweight kid, from a single parent home. Poor, overweight, and fragile makes for an easy target in the jungle that is the older grades of elementary school. There were bullies that were harassing at times. This led me to develop this Incredible Hulk type response to criticism and negativity. I found out if you just blew up and lost your temper, let people know you were crazy if pushed too far, they'd leave you alone. The problem is this leads to adulthood, and now you're a 25 year old man with this quick temper.

So what is the path forward? Psalm 139:23-24 says, "Search me, O God, and know my heart: try me, and know my thoughts: And see if there be any wicked way in me, and lead me in the way everlasting." (KJV) Ask God to search us and relieve any hidden, underlying causes in our lives. This may be a painful experience. It could cause us to relive some painful memories, but this search is necessary.

Recently I had some blood work come back a little off. The doctors ran tests, did an MRI, and an ultrasound. Ultimately this searching revealed an inflamed gallbladder full of gallstones. I didn't have the classic gallbladder attack symptoms, but this was the underlying cause of my issue. The doctors had to dig, they had to search it out. This is much the same way we need the Lord to search us and find the underlying cause of the issue.

You have to let the light of the Lord illuminate your life. The closer you get to God the more the light shines into the dark nooks and crannies of our soul. It shines past the surface and easy to see spots, into the depths. Ruth Graham once told a story about a news crew coming to the house she and Billy Graham lived in. The crew wanted to do an interview, and she busied herself with cleaning until everything was spotless. When the crew arrived they brought in large lights to make sure everything was perfect for the broadcast. She was appalled when these lights revealed dust and little cobwebs in far corners of the room. Nobody noticed but her. She came to understand, the more light you put in the room, the more you notice things that were once invisible to the naked eye. Additionally, when we allow the light of the Lord to shine brightly upon us, He will show us the cobwebs in the corner. The underlying issues that need correction.

Kill the roots, kill the fruits. If you want the fruit to disappear, in my case anger was the fruit, then you must allow God to take care of the roots. The roots are strongholds in our life. Hard places that are well protected. They are firmly established, set in. 2 Corinthians 10:4 states, "For the weapons of our warfare are not carnal but mighty to the pulling down of strongholds." (NKJV) Just to be clear, we have talked about some of these weapons, but it's good to repeat. I see the weapons as seven different spiritual disciplines or practices. These are reading the Bible, praying, fasting, worship, sharing our testimony, speaking the name of Jesus, and thanksgiving. Fill your life with these things, and you'll be amazed as strongholds fall in your life.

Reflection

1. Why do you think the root issues of our struggles are so much more painful to work though than the surface issues that are easily seen?

2. Reflect on the weapons of our warfare. What weapons do you use readily? Which of the seven could use a little more use? Can you think of any other spiritual weapons?

3. Have you prayed recently and asked the Lord to search your heart? Search the depths? Let's ask God to illuminate any way in us that isn't of Him.

LESSON #27
MEMENTO MORI

"When it comes your time to die, be not like those whose hearts are filled with fear of death, so that when their time comes they weep and pray for a little more time to live their lives over again in a different way. Sing your death song and die like a hero going home."

— CHIEF TECUMSEH

My friend Boxcar and I share a mutual love of pushing ourselves in endurance type events. I enjoy these type events more than any big guy should. I ran a marathon weighing nearly 240 lbs. The knees and ankles bear the brunt of our crazy ideas. This is what led us to a trail run back in 2021.

This particular run was in a park that connected with a portion of the Florida Trail. Boxcar found the event, and it happened to be a never ending loop race, which is my favorite type of race. If you are unfamiliar, a never ending loop is a race with a set course, this one was about five miles. You run this five mile course repeatedly until you can't continue. I did twenty-five miles this race, just shy of a second marathon distance. Not too bad for a big ole boy.

As we weaved through the course, and interacted with the Florida Trail, I noticed something strange about one of the orange blazes. There was an orange blaze on a post marking the Florida Trail. Written in black marker in the middle of the orange blaze were two latin words, "Memento Mori." I stopped and took a picture of this interesting trail marker. I'm looking back at the picture now on my phone. It's very meaningful to me, perhaps you know the meaning of the latin phrase, if not, I'll teach you. It basically means "remember you will die."

There is a whole segment of artistic expression from antiquity that commemorates the phrase. It has its roots in classical Christianity. If you've ever seen a classic artwork of someone writing or going through their daily work, and it has a skull or hourglass in the picture, then you've seen Memento Mori art. Some frown upon such expressions today. We really don't do clothes or items with skulls on them in our house. However, this was looked at differently for early Christians. Skulls were a reminder of mortality, a reminder to live on the straight and narrow, because we will all die. Early Puritan settlers often had Memento Mori images on their tombstones as a warning to those left behind. Death is coming, what are you doing with your life?

I've been accused of thinking about death more than I should. My family already knows my wishes for my funeral if something were to happen to me. They vetoed the idea of floating my body down the river and setting me afire with a flaming arrow. That was my first choice. Too many legalities to deal with, and Michelle was vehemently against the idea. Funny thoughts aside, I do subscribe to habit #2 from Franklin Covey's seven habits. I begin each day with the end in mind. I realize I'm on the clock, I've got to bring more laborers into the outdoors ministry, this work has to outlive the workers we have now. I'm like a farmer staring at a field ripe for harvest, knowing there will come a day when I can no longer do the work, knowing there will come a day when it's all gone. I have today, and I must do everything I can, with the time I have, to get the crop in.

One problem for most people is we don't think about the end until we're blindsided by a doctor's report on a random Tuesday. We think we're going to be here forever, going to our jobs forever, pastoring our churches for thirty more years. We preach about the end all the time, but we're often not living intentionally. We are guilty of going through the motions, and years slip by. Then, when the bad report hits us, we are filled with regret, wishing we had more time, going through the bucket list items. You see, the time is now. Go ride the bull, zipline, share Jesus with your neighbor, preach like a dying man to dying men and women. Remember you will die, you don't have forever, the time is now.

Bonnie Ware, a palliative care specialist, wrote a book entitled, *The Top Five Regrets of Dying - A Life Transformed by the Dearly Departing*. I will list them here for you.

1. "I wish I'd had the courage to live a life true to myself, not the life others expected of me."
2. "I wish I hadn't worked so hard."

3. "I wish I'd had the courage to express my
   feelings."
4. "I wish I had stayed in touch with my friends."
5. "I wish that I'd let myself be happier."[1]

If you do the research you will find several of these lists. I think Bonnie Ware's list sums it up best. The most common regret at death was the failure to follow through on a dream or calling.

I write in coffee shops and shared work spaces all over. I have noticed there are several people who frequent the same coffee shops for writing. Recently, I was talking with a lady I've run into many times during the course of writing two books. She and I compete for the best corners in the same shops, but we've developed a friendship. She's retired, I'd guess around seventy, and she's working diligently on her first novel. It's a historical fiction work set during the Civil War. She was telling me that she always wanted to write a book. Then she got married, had kids, went to work, and did all the things life required. The dream of writing a book was placed on the backburner. Now, after all these years, she has finally written a book. She followed her dream. I told her how much I admired her following her dream. So few people do that.

The second most common regret listed is wishing they didn't spend so much time at work. I touched on this in my first book. I admonish parents not to miss the kids' ball games trying to pay for all the bigger and better toys we love to acquire. I understand we have to work and make a living. The old saying, "Don't be so worried about making a living, you forget to make a life." Everywhere I go people come up to me and tell me how much they'd love to have hiked on the Appalachian Trail, but it's too late now. For some it is truly too late, it's irresponsible for me to encourage someone to go hike clearly past their ability to do so. My heart aches a little for these folks, I see it in their eyes, life moves so fast, sometimes it passes us by.

As a Christian our life is built of the pursuits we have in this life, and hope we have in the next. Often, we can feel overwhelmed thinking of death, because we only focus on this life. This life is not the end, this is only the beginning. We are spiritual beings having a human experience. Christ muted the pain of death when he overcame death, hell, and the grave. Paul writes in 1 Corinthians 15, "Death, where is your sting? Grave, where is your victory?" To know Christ as Savior is to know peace in the face of eternity. Death is a promotion to a life our finite minds can't comprehend.

Too often we focus on the length of life, and fail to focus on the depth of life. How pointless to have a long life, full of empty mundane pursuits, with no depth. We gain depth by filling our lives with things that have meaning and purpose. In one of my favorite sermons John Piper shared his thoughts on having one life, and not wasting it. He shared the story of Ruby Elison and Laura Edwards having been killed in Cameroon, Africa. Two ladies in their 80's who died sharing Jesus. He asks, "Is this a tragedy?" Then he reads this story from *Reader's Digest*.

Piper says, "I will tell you what a tragedy is. I will show you how to waste your life. Consider a story from the February 1998 edition of *Reader's Digest*, which tells about a couple who "took early retirement from their jobs in the Northeast five years ago when he was 59 and she was 51.

Now they live in Punta Gorda, Florida, where they cruise on their 30 foot trawler, play softball and collect seashells."

At first, when I read it I thought it might be a joke. A spoof on the American Dream. But it wasn't. Tragically, this was the dream: Come to the end of your life- your one and only precious, God-given life- and let the last great work of your life, before you give an account to your creator, be this: playing softball and collecting seashells.

Picture them before Christ on the great day of judgment: 'Look, Lord. See my shells.' That is a tragedy. And people today are spending billions of dollars to persuade you to embrace that tragic dream. Over against that, I put my protest: Don't buy it. Don't waste your life."[2]

If only someone who reads this, wakes up and realizes this is your one precious life. What are you doing with it? God has given you this one opportunity, don't waste it. I'll leave you with the words of the great missionary C.T. Studd:

<blockquote>
Two little lines I heard one day,
Traveling along life's busy way;
Bringing conviction to my heart,
And from my mind would not depart;
Only one life, 'twill soon be past,
Only what's done for Christ will last.[3]
</blockquote>

<u>Reflection</u>

1. Do you have an unfulfilled dream? What are some steps you can take to see it come to pass?
2. What are your thoughts on the sermon excerpt from John Piper? (You can access the whole sermon through various online sites.)
3. How does the pace of life negatively affect our depth of life?

LESSON #28
GOD'S WAY IS BETTER

Jesus replied, "You don't understand now what I'm doing, but someday you will."

— JOHN 13:7 NLT

I recently had a friend who went hiking and he took some great pictures. One picture stood out to me, as well as his caption underneath the photo. I'll try to explain it to you.

My friend's photo was of a stream crossing, it had a man made bridge, but that bridge had been washed out by a storm. What was left of the footbridge was still visible in the water, but it had sunk. Now, hikers were using a fallen tree limb to cross the stream, and it was doing a great job. The natural God provided option was handling the work where the man made structure had failed. I couldn't help but think how true this is in our everyday lives.

For starters, we must trust God has more information to solve our problems than we do. I am the master of trying to handle every problem in my own strength and power. I'll sit and think through the issue, I'll rehash the problem, I'll calculate all the variables of information, and I'll attempt to come up with a solution. That's not bad, that's sound decision making 101. Here's the issue. No matter how much I know about the given situation, God knows more. In Isaiah 55:8-9 we read, "For my thoughts are not your thoughts, neither are your ways my ways, declares the Lord. As the heavens are higher than the earth, so are my ways higher than your ways and my thoughts than your thoughts." (NIV) I choose to trust the Lord with my problems because He has all the information. The door He opens is the right door, and the door He shuts is the right door.

Here's another story for illustration. Our family drove to all the different trail towns near the Appalachian Trail when trying to decide where to home base. We looked in Erwin, TN and near Franklin, NC. We drove through Damascus, VA and Hot Springs, NC. We checked out Front Royal, VA, Boiling Springs, PA, and Gorham, NH. Never, not one time, did Shady Valley, TN come up. It wasn't on our radar, it wasn't technically one of the well known trail towns. We prayed about where to go, and visited with realtors in these different towns. We juggled pros and cons of each location, considered prices for our limited budget, and thought about the winters in each place. We didn't even know Shady Valley existed. You hike right by it on the trail; most hikers don't even know this little valley is there, but all along God had the perfect place in mind for us.

I remember we decided we wanted to be near Damascus, VA. It is Trail Town USA. Several trails converge here, and it's home to Trail Days each year the weekend after Mother's Day. It was the perfect spot, but the prices in the area caused houses in town to remain out of reach. We decided to look in the outlying areas, and that's how we ran across a local real estate agent. She tried her best to find us the perfect property, but nothing worked. Some areas were very remote, no internet, no septic, and no cell service. I've mentioned our wishlist earlier in Lesson 16. This was impossible. Then the Lord worked it out. Why Shady Valley? The Lord had the information I didn't have.

I later learned many towns have regulations on allowing hikers to camp on your property in town. I did not know this at the time we were looking for property. Had we bought something in certain towns, we would have been heavily regulated on how we could interact with hikers. Also, close neighbors in town tend to frown on certain activities, like outdoor showers for hikers. What the Lord did was place us in Shady Valley with fewer neighbors and very few regulations dealing with hikers camping on our property. We can have a bunkhouse, outdoor showers, pole barns, and campers on the lot. We can have a firepit, and stay up talking into the wee hours of the morning. The Lord had the information I didn't have. He knew what we needed, and where we needed it. I spent time worrying about something He was taking care of the whole time. How often do we do that?

I have a sermon I've preached called "Just because we don't understand doesn't mean God has no plan." It's taken from the first couple chapters of Exodus when the children of Israel are enslaved. No doubt they questioned the years of captivity, they questioned the persecution, and maybe wondered what God was doing. Here is what I see God doing in hindsight.

First, He was protecting and growing this small nation. When they first went to Egypt they were just one small family. A small family of less than 100 could have been overrun by thieves and robbers, but Egypt protected them unaware. By the time they were freed, the once small nation was most likely well over 1.5 million strong.

Then, God protected them morally. Egypt was far from righteous, but they were far better than the neighboring Canaanites. They didn't have to worry about moral failure due to assimilation because the Egyptians looked down on the Hebrews. They saw the occupation of shepherding as lowly and repulsive. They'd never intermarry with them.

Finally, God strengthened and prepared them for the journey ahead. The Hebrews were a force to be reckoned with by the time they fled captivity. They had been hardened by the furnace of adversity. They were made strong in the brick pits, and by the building projects of Egypt.

I think back to those summer football practices. The heat and adversity we went through together. Our coaches knew if you suffer through a hard time together you become much stronger as a unit. You'll fight for each other. You'll win because of the people on your left and right. That's what God was doing. The Hebrews were protected, kept pure, and made strong while in captivity. We don't always know what God is doing, but we have to trust His plan is better than our plan.

<u>Reflection</u>

1. Think back on a time when the Lord worked out a situation for you that you couldn't work out on your own.
2. How does knowing God is in control help us through troubling times?
3. What is your favorite Verse dealing with the subject of trusting the Lord?

LESSON #29
THE LITTLE THINGS

"It's the little details that are vital. Little things make big things happen."

— JOHN WOODEN

I get asked all the time what I'm most afraid of in the woods. I know the answers that are expected. People want to hear about bears, coyotes, snakes, and alligators. Perhaps, a mountain lion or Bigfoot. These are always the big topics of discussion, and I always answer the same. The thing I fear the most are ticks. Yes, those little creepy crawlers are the only things that cost me sleep in the woods.

I enjoy cowboy camping. This involves little setup, just you camping on the ground with your sleeping bag right in the open. If I'm cowboy camping I try to find an area away from bushes, and I usually like it to be in a colder season, because I know ticks are out more in warmer times, and they like to hang out in thicker brush. I do not like ticks for several reasons. One, I'm not a fan of bugs biting me and drinking my blood. Two, these bugs carry a variety of diseases that can do major harm to the body.

Every year I meet hikers who have had to get off trail somewhere in Virginia, or Pennsylvania, and take medicine to counter Lyme disease. They can eventually return to their hike if they caught it in time. Lyme disease is tricky to determine, and you have to be very watchful.

Once while in PennMar Park, on the border of Maryland and Pennsylvania, Meredith got a tick on her. We had set up a trail blessing there. This park is one of the places on trail you can call and have a pizza delivered to you. They deliver it right to your picnic table. It's a great place for people to stop and take a break, so we set up here. The park has berry bushes, and Meredith loves to pick berries when we see them, so she had been in the bushes. On the way home she asks, "What is this on me?" I knew immediately it was a tick, and we carefully got it off her, making sure to remove the whole head. It had already attached, so that wasn't good. However, we knew it could only have been there an hour or two at most. Typically it takes longer for a tick to spread the different tick borne viruses to a human. We did what we knew to do. We marked the spot and prayed over it. You mark it because Lyme disease has a red ring that will develop around the bite mark in a couple days. It looks like a bullseye. If you get the bullseye that's bad, if not, you're in the clear. The area we were in near Maryland has a much higher occurrence rate of Lyme disease than any areas in southern Appalachia, but Meredith was good. Praise the Lord for that.

It's amazing how ticks are such small creatures, but they can cause the most trouble. I'll tell you another experience. I met a guy near the trail. He wasn't a hiker, but a traveler. He had been experiencing some worrisome issues with his health. I encouraged him to return home and work to rebuild the relationship with his parents, which he did. Later, his doctors figured out some of his health issues were related to untreated Lyme disease.

For me, one of the most dreaded species of ticks is the Lone Star tick. This tick is active in the southeast and has a white dot on its back. The major concern with it is the meat allergy can be common with its bite. This can leave you unable to eat red meat without getting extremely sick. I have met one person with this allergy. I can't imagine not being able to eat a steak.

Song of Solomon 2:15 gives us an interesting passage of Scripture. It says, "Take the foxes, The little foxes that spoil the vines, For our vines have tender grapes." Those little pesky things we so often ignore can cause the most damage. To fully understand the imagery we need to understand the way foxes and deer eat grapes. The larger animals, like deer, would come and eat the grapes from the hanging branches. Foxes are small and can't reach the hanging branches, so they gnaw the vines themselves near the bottom. This kills the vine and causes the grapes to fall to the ground where they can get to them.

We can't ignore the "small things" in life. The little things will make or break you. I always caution addicts about leaving doors of temptation open in their lives. Perhaps you used to be addicted to meth, now you just dip snuff. Will that snuff send you to hell? That seems like an okay trade off, right? I'll tell you what it does. It's a little fox that keeps the door of addiction open in your life, and if you aren't careful you'll find yourself right back in a worse situation. So many people end up in a relapsed state because we can't keep the little foxes out of the garden.

You want to know what breaks up churches? It's not a fist fight free for all on Sunday morning, although I've heard of it happening. It's a little gossip, a little backbiting, a little pride, a little offense you just can't let go. Those little foxes eventually bring down the whole vine, and these little things will eventually bring trouble to the church. You can't give place to sin, no matter how small you perceive it to be.

Charles Spurgeon once said, "Little things lead to big things." This is true both good and bad. A little splinter, left unchecked, under the skin can lead to a great infection. Those little sins, the ones we have retained, so small the world barely notices, will eventually cause you the most problems. They will fester, they will cause rot, they will lead to pain. Get the splinter out as quickly as possible.

It's amazing to think the bite of a small tick could take your life if left untreated, but it's a great warning at the same time. Those little things can cause us so many issues if we allow them to grow. Think about the best way to combat the tick - daily observation of the outside of your body. If you catch it quickly you are usually good. Likewise, taking a daily account of our heart can help keep us free from the spiritual pests that seek to harm and destroy.

<u>Reflection</u>

1. In what ways can "little things" be more detrimental than "big things?"
2. What happens to our Christian walk when we attempt to retain our "pet sins?"
3. Did the explanation of how the foxes destroy the vines bring new light to our fight against the enemy?

LESSON #30
NEXT

"The reward you get for overcoming your last challenge is your next challenge."

— T.D. JAKES

Each year I meet many people who conquer the Appalachian Trail, and the question is always, "What's next?" You'd be amazed at the number of people who already have the next challenge lined up. People plan on heading to Colorado, or Arizona to hike the long trails in those states. Some will continue on towards Canada on the International Appalachian Trail - how many of you knew that even existed? Some will return to jobs and careers, let's not pretend this won't be a challenge. It's a fact of life, there will be another mountain.

An Evangelist friend likes to say we are all either pre-mess, mid-mess, or post-mess about to get into more trouble. Challenges are part of the cycle of life. On this side of heaven we will all have obstacles to face. If this book does nothing else, I hope it helps you to face those daily struggles. My goal in life is to point people towards Jesus, because he is our help, our strength, our stronghold.

I was given a copy of my great-grandfather's obituary. He was part of the early church planting work near Ariton, and was a friend of Jim and Dan Dubose, sometimes traveling and speaking with them. He contracted pneumonia and died at 31 years of age. His final recorded words to his young family was, "Keep your eyes fixed on Jesus, he will carry you through."

The next challenge is coming, like it or not. How will we make it? I'll leave you with these words. We have to keep our eyes fixed on Jesus, he will carry you over the next mountain.

"Where Roads Don't Go"
By Brad Sasser

O to be where roads don't go,
Where trout swim upstream 'neath cold winter snow,
Where deer run free, and wild rivers flow,
O to be where roads don't go.
We hike along mountains zigging to and fro,
Our burdens in packs, backs weighed down low,
The pace is steady, spring grasses they grow,
O to be where roads don't go.
Marching along, disregard status quo,
When the clock stops, nobody can know,
But I pass with a smile, let my wrinkles show,
'Cause I spent my life where roads don't go.

ACKNOWLEDGEMENTS

I owe a special thanks to my volunteer editors Elaine Rieben, Rachel Rieben, and William Hurst. These individuals make me look better than I am and I appreciate them immensely.

Thank you to everyone who enjoyed the first book and encouraged me to write another. I won't be on the New York Times bestseller list, but I'm pretty sure I made the Clayton Record's list.

Where would I be without my wonderful wife and kids? They always allowed me time to write, and pushed me to chase these dreams. I love you guys.

Words fall short to thank our numerous partners and churches who faithfully support our work financially and through prayer.

A special thanks to everyone who has come to help with the projects at the lot in Shady Valley. I love each one of you.

ABOUT THE AUTHOR

Brad Sasser has dedicated his life to the Lord's service for the past fifteen years. He's been a Youth Pastor, Pastor, and US Missionary.

He, alongside his wife Michelle, and their two children, Lane (17) and Meredith (14), currently serves as a Chaplain to Outdoor enthusiasts.

They travel the long trails of America, showing the love of Christ to the hurting.

NOTES

LESSON #1

1. English Standard Version
2. NKJV
3. MEV
4. https://www.wcnc.com/article/news/local/wake-up-charlotte/stressed-worrying-is-a-waste-of-your-time-experts-say/275-517236ed-b890-4cba-b671-827911a87f9f

LESSON #2

1. Norbury, James. *Big Panda and Tiny Dragon*. Mandala Publishing, 2021.

LESSON #3

1. Appalachian Trail Conservancy https://appalachiantrail.org/our-work/about-us/media-room/#:~:text=How%20many%20people%20use%20the,of%20those%20completing%20the%20Trail.
2. Blog.adioma.com "Why we live-Counting the People Your Life Impacts."

LESSON #5

1. Tyndale, New Living Translation

LESSON #6

1. Fly Fishing Flies and Their Uses. http://drifthook.com/blogs/discover/fly-fishing-flies-and-their-uses

LESSON #8

1. https://dianaleaghmatthews.com/whever-he-leads/#.Y8V3_qRMFPw

LESSON #10

1. https://www.linkedin.com/pulse/we-can-roll-over-give-up-like-john-stephen-akhwari-macro-n%C3%BA%C3%B1ez-yur%c3%A9n

LESSON #11

1. Tyndale House Publishers. (2015). Holy Bible: New Living Translation

LESSON #14

1. https://www.theforestacademy.com/tree-knowledge/annual-growth-rings/#.Y9qWuqRMFPw
2. Jonathan Edwards. *A Divine and Supernatural Light, Immediately Imparted to the Soul by the Spirit of God, Shown to be Both Scriptural and Rational Doctrine*. Curiosmith, 2012.

LESSON #18

1. https://thefellowship.org/soul-stir/punching-holes-in-the-darkness/#:~:text=Robert%20Louis%20Stevenson%20was%20an,punching%20holes%20in%20the%20darkness%E2%80%9

LESSON #19

1. Mark Mittelberg. *Contagious Faith: Discover Your Natural Style For Sharing Jesus With Others*. Zondervan. Oct. 2021

LESSON #20

1. www.inc.com/jeff-haden/the-1-in-60-rule-how-remarkably-success-ful-people-stay-on-track-to-accomplish-their-biggest-goals.html#:~:text=That's%20why%20pilots%20are%20taught,out%20to%20be%

LESSON #21

1. The importance of human connection- CMHA National. https://cmha.ca/news/the-importance-of-human-connection/#:~:text=But%20connecting%20with%20others%20is,put%20our%20health%20at%20risk.

LESSON #23

1. Daniel Pink. *The Power of Regret*. Riverhead Books. Feb. 1, 2022.

LESSON #27

1. Bonnie Ware. *The Top Five Regrets of the Dying: A Life Transformed by the Dearly Departing*. Hay House. 2011
2. John Piper. *Don't Waste Your Life*. Crossway. 2003
3. Only One Life, 'Twill Soon Be Past by C.T. Studd